INSIDER CRIME –
THE NEW LAW

INSIDER CRIME – THE NEW LAW

Dr Barry Rider
Dean and Tutor of Jesus College
Cambridge

Michael Ashe
Barrister of the Middle Temple and King's Inns, Dublin

JORDANS

1993

Published by
Jordan Publishing Ltd
21 St Thomas Street
Bristol BS1 6JS

British Library Cataloguing-in-Publication Data
A catalogue record for this book is available from the British Library.

ISBN 0 85308 218 9

Photoset by Rowland Phototypesetting Ltd, Bury St Edmunds, Suffolk
Printed by Henry Ling Ltd, The Dorset Press, Dorchester

PREFACE

Contrary to what some people may think (including one or two of our friends) we do not consider insider dealing as the most serious of the 'white collar' offences, let alone criminal offences. As we have reflected about insider dealing over the years, we have become less and less convinced that it is the heinous and immoral act which it is often represented to be. To devote one's life and work to the pursuit of the insider, as some people appear to have done, does not immediately commend itself when the subject is seen in the wider context of fraud.

Insider dealing or, shall we expose our prejudice and say, insider abuse, is, of course, a matter of concern because it does tend to throw into stark contrast those members of our society who are, or who appear to be, on the inside track compared to others in less privileged positions. Whether, dislike of these insiders is motivated by a burning passion to see equality reign supreme in those markets which are inherently unequal, or whether, as we suspect, it is motivated by rather more basic instincts, we leave to the discerning reader. However, the fact is that the debate, at least for the time being, is over as to whether and in what form the law should intervene.

With the enactment of the Criminal Justice Act 1993, we now have a new and, in some respects, radical set of provisions which have terrorised the City and may yet live up to the worst fears of those imaginative City lawyers who have gone to such extremes in convincing their clients not to fret. Who has, after all, ever met a lawyer who was willing to persuade his client that he did not have a problem?

Whilst we are, more or less, convinced that no one, who would not have been in jeopardy under the old law, will be hauled before the Crown Court under the new law, this is not the end of the story. The criminal law does not operate in a vacuum. There are, irrespective of what the Act may say, civil implications of insider crime. These may be either disciplinary or involve financial liability at law.

The civil law may impose liability for various forms of insider dealing and, in recent years, the courts in England and elsewhere have shown a willingness to search out 'crooks' and give them their just deserts. For example, in a recent decision of the Court of Appeal of New South Wales, Mahony JA observed that the time-honoured rule that a director owed no duties of disclosure to shareholders with whom he was dealing, reflected a morality of a bygone age when the use of inside information was more or less a legitimate expectation and perk of management. Furthermore, the impact of rules and practices promulgated by the various self-regulatory organisations must be considered, not only in terms of their own disciplinary jurisdiction but, in the context of prospective derivative civil liability. In this book, we have attempted, in a practical and hopefully helpful manner, to address these and other issues within both the narrow and wider contexts of insider crime.

Subject to implementation, the law is as stated on the 1 November 1993. Inevitably, these are areas of law and regulation which are fast moving and it is never entirely possible to predict every development even in the immediate future. Indeed, between the preparation of galley and page proofs of this book, the Australian decision, to which mention has already been made, was handed down; the Government published proposals on timely disclosure; and The Stock Exchange published its amended Listings Rules containing the Model Code on insider dealing. None the less, with the assistance of Jordans, we have attempted to do our best in this regard.

BARRY RIDER
Jesus College
Cambridge

MICHAEL ASHE
Lincoln's Inn
London

CONTENTS

r-7

PART 3   CIVIL LIABILITY AND ENFORCEMENT

APPENDICES

TABLE OF CASES

Table of US Cases

TABLE OF STATUTES

TABLE OF AUSTRALIAN STATUTES

TABLE OF US STATUTES

TABLE OF STATUTORY INSTRUMENTS

TABLE OF ABBREVIATIONS

CJA 1993	Criminal Justice Act 1993
FSA 1986	Financial Services Act 1986
IMRO	Investment Management Regulatory Organisation
Model Code	The Stock Exchange's Model Code on conduct for securities transactions by directors of listed companies
NASDAQ	National Association of Securities Dealers Automated Quotations System
OM (London)	Swedish Options Market
RPB	recognised professional body
SEC	US Securities and Exchange Commission
SFO	Serious Fraud Office
SIB	Securities and Investments Board
Yellow Book	The Listing Rules

PART 1

BACKGROUND TO THE LEGISLATION

INTRODUCTION

Public perception of insider dealing

To many, if not most people, the phrase 'insider dealing' conjures up a picture of a slick and rather smooth 'City-type' making a 'killing' on The Stock Exchange on the basis of a 'tip' some chum of his has given him over lunch. As with most popular impressions, this picture has an element of justification and a good deal of prejudice. To the extent that many of us consider such conduct objectionable, one wonders if this is from a reaction of jealousy rather than from any deep-seated moral, let alone rational, principle. It is true that in the US, and to some degree elsewhere, a significant proportion of serious cases of insider abuse come to the attention of the authorities, not through the sophisticated endeavours and diligence of 'stock watch units', but because someone 'grouses'. Indeed, the Chief Litigation Counsel of the US Securities and Exchange Commission (SEC) has observed,[1] not entirely tongue in cheek, that the enforcement role of his Division would have been far less impressive without the aid of hurt wives, disappointed and jilted lovers, disgruntled employees and jealous colleagues. In fact, the SEC considered this so important in policing insider dealing that US Congress, at the urging of the SEC, introduced a provision in the Insider Trading and Securities Fraud Enforcement Act 1988 empowering the SEC to pay 'bounties' to informants.[2] The House of Commons' Select Committee on Trade and Industry[3] considered whether such an approach would be useful in the UK. However, whilst some members of the Committee inclined to the prospect of 'bounty hunters' in the Square Mile, it was generally thought to be a little too American!

Traditionally, insider abuse has involved individuals who are connected with the management of companies, rather than the smooth operators conjured up in the popular press. Of course, this is not to say that, in fact, the incidence of insider abuse is not greater in regard to those who operate in the financial services industry and relevant professions than in the more easily identifiable relationships of management and ownership. To some extent what is considered to be insider dealing will be influenced by the philosophical basis upon which it is sought to distinguish such conduct (invariably as an object of opprobrium) from other 'normal' conduct. For the ordinary man in the street, who has neither the opportunity nor the desire to contemplate the outpourings of academics and others on this much discussed topic, insider dealing can be described as involving the deliberate exploitation of information by dealing in securities, or other property, to which the information relates, having obtained that information by virtue of some privileged relationship or position. In other words, insider dealing involves 'taking advantage' of an opportunity to profit which is not available to others and from whom, directly or indirectly, the profit will be taken.

Historical background

Insider dealing, in the wider sense of 'taking advantage' of privileged information to the disadvantage of those who have had no opportunity to acquire such insight, is nothing new. History and, indeed, mythology are replete with examples of individuals 'taking advantage' of information which only they have been given access to. The gift of 'greater knowledge' or insight was counted as a blessing[4] and certainly brought no disgrace to those who benefited by its use over those ill-informed and dispossessed. Such criticism as was recorded tended to fasten upon the status of the informant or 'tipper', than on the use which the 'tippee' made of it. Thus, if the source was good, in whatever sense was vogue, the application of the privilege was a blessing not to be faulted or questioned. Sadly, today, things are not so black and white and the modern 'tippee' may find that those charged with administering the Criminal Justice Act 1993 (CJA 1993) are less reverential.

Commissioners appointed by the English Parliament reported in November 1696[5] that they had discovered conduct, which amounted to insider manipulation and trading, of such a nature as to 'pervert the end and design of companies'. The Commissioners considered that this was undermining the 'Trade of England' and, whilst legislation directly relevant to insider abuse took almost 300 years to materialise, as a result of their concern Parliament began to legislate against the 'pernicious art of stock-jobbing'.[6] On 8 February 1872, *The Commercial and Financial Chronicle* stated that the manipulation of inside information by directors and officers of companies was 'a very great evil'. Therefore, according to the editor, those who took advantage of their position to control the timing of disclosures of information which could be expected to affect the price of securities were deserving of public criticism and censure. It is more difficult to discover references to the iniquity of simply taking advantage of information which comes into a person's possession by virtue of employment or position and where there is no manipulation of events. Sir Winston Churchill considered an allegation in *The Financial News*, that he had taken advantage of inside information during the Marconi scandal, as 'downright insulting and libellous'.[7] As the century progressed and, to paraphrase Sir Edward Heath,[8] the unacceptable face of capitalism became more exposed, insider abuse was condemned in even stronger terms. The last Lord Chief Justice had no qualms in branding it 'cheating'.[9] Such an epithet, however, whilst it is one with which the authors wholly agree, raises rather more questions than it answers.

The policy of regulation

One must look, albeit briefly,[10] at the policy justifications for regulating insider dealing. The effectiveness of insider regulation, supposing that regulation is desirable, must be determined in the light of the policy selected for justifying intervention in the first place.[11]

Whilst it is rare to find positive support for insider dealing outside the ranks of those seeking to justify a brand of economic liberalism which would embarrass 'Captain Morgan' let alone 'Captain Bob',[12] it is difficult to identify, in any empirical way, the harm which insider dealing is thought to cause. Indeed, despite all the literature and the promotion of an international anti-insider dealing crusade by the SEC little is really known about the incidents, character and quality of insider abuse. Like so many forms of questionable or questioned conduct in the financial and business sector, the picture is unclear. The incidents which are apparent tend to be thrown up, if not by accident, then by events unrelated to the systematic procedures that have been created for detection.[13] Hence, the notion exists, rightly or wrongly, that what is seen or even perceived is only the tip of the iceberg. To adopt another metaphor, one might assume that there are insider traders in the market in the same way that, where there is long grass, one might assume the presence of elephants – at least in Africa!

Professor Henry Manne[14] (in what is generally regarded as the most convincing defence of insider trading), referring to the widespread view that insider dealing is unfair, equated this 'unscientific' approach to one of his young law students stamping [their] foot and stating 'I don't care: it's just not right'.[15] Fairness is a well-known and cherished concept, but one which is difficult to rationalise or to use as a reliable tool for creating, as opposed to fashioning, rights. Furthermore, it is often pointed out, at least in anonymous market transactions, that the person who happens to deal with the insider, usually as a consequence of random matching of orders, is a willing purchaser or seller at the market price at that point in time. He is in no way misled by the insider. So where is the unfairness to this person?

Is it not unfair that the insider has taken advantage of information or an opportunity which has come to him by virtue of his position or through some privileged relationship? Generally, we do not regard the mere taking of a benefit as unfair unless there is some kind of demonstrable harm.[16] It is difficult to perceive that harm has been done to the person with whom, by chance, the insider deals, and it is equally hard to perceive that harm, in the majority of cases, has been done to the owner of the information or controller of the insider's status. Thus, whilst Professor Loss[17] observes that one might consider the young student's retort somewhat healthier than the scepticism of that student's professor, it is difficult to justify insider regulation simply on the basis that it is unfair to the person with whom the insider deals.

It could be argued (and has been – particularly in North America) that insider dealing harms the proper interests of the corporate issuer in whose shares the insider dealing takes place.[18] Where the person who takes advantage of the information in question is also a director or officer or is in some other clearly defined relationship involving confidence and trust within the company, the potential for harm is considered to be even greater. A company which has acquired the reputation of being an 'insiders' company will, it is contended by proponents of this view, have difficulty in securing finance on competitive terms. The company will also suffer in the market as a consequence of loss of respect in the integrity of its management.[19] It is also argued that, if insider dealing is permitted, there will be a temptation for those responsible for ensuring prompt disclosure of price-sensitive information to delay or manipulate such disclosures.[20] The courts have been prepared to accept that the harm caused to issuers by such conduct justifies legal liability. In reality, however, most of these arguments are somewhat academic and insubstantial.

Perhaps a more telling justification of legal liability is the notion that where a person in a position of trust abuses the confidence that has been reposed in him, it is right and proper that he should be required to yield up any benefit that he has obtained by virtue of this breach of duty.[21] The harm is in the breach of trust and specific damage beyond this is not required. Whilst such an approach is appropriate in relation to what the law regards as fiduciaries, the vast majority of those likely to be involved in insider trading will not be in a traditional, fiduciary relationship.[22] It would seem appropriate to justify control of insider dealing on this basis only in situations where there is a pre-existing relationship of stewardship and, thus, an implicit obligation of trust. Thus, the fiduciary approach would justify depriving insiders who are fiduciaries of their unauthorised profits, but would be of limited application.[23] Another approach is to regard the information as 'belonging' to the issuer of the securities or some other party who has a proper interest in a person not using the information for his or another's personal and unauthorised gain.[24] According to this notion, insider trading involves a misappropriation, or almost a theft, of the inside information or the opportunity to exploit that information.[25] To some extent this approach merely moves the debate into determining what information is considered capable of being misappropriated and in which circumstances this will arise. As a general rule, it is only where an individual is under a duty of some kind not to misuse the information that it can sensibly be argued that his taking advantage of it amounts to a misappropriation. In practical terms, this limits the approach to cases of definite fiduciary obligation. However, it is conceivable to attach the obligation to the information itself, provided that those who receive it do so in circumstances where, because of their knowledge that it is communicated to them in breach of an obligation, there is a fiduciary obligation not to misuse it.[26] In practice, however, given the underdeveloped jurisprudence in England, relating to information as property, this approach is fraught with difficulty.

It is argued that the primary justification for insider dealing regulation is equality of information for those in the market.[27] Whilst this notion comports with the proper desire to draw into the market as much information as possible to allow investors to reach informed and sensible decisions, it has been criticised as being naive. It has been observed, not just by cynics, that many investment decisions are made because the investor considers that he has superior information. Indeed, the efficient market hypothesis, for what it is worth,[28] would argue that substantial profits can only be made, on a regular basis, on information which is not available to the market. Furthermore, why should it be necessary for such information to be disclosed in the context of securities' transactions when it has always been assumed that there is no similar merit in dealings on other markets?[29] Furthermore, it may be more sensible, in order to achieve equality of information, to require issuers to make timely disclosure[30] of all material events as a matter of law, rather than to seek equality through the random penalising of those who take advantage of informational imbalances.[31] Some would also argue, perhaps with questionable empirical support, that insider dealing is a reasonably effective and economic means of drawing such information into the market, both through direct intervention in the market and induced trading.[32]

In the view of the authors, however, no matter how appealing these, and the legion of other, arguments seem,[33] the main (if not only) convincing justification for controlling insider dealing is that it has a perceived, adverse impact on confidence. It does not matter, according to this view, whether insider dealing has a detrimental effect on the operation of the markets or the fortunes of issuers because, if enough opinion-forming individuals consider that it is wrong (*apropos* Professor Manne's foot-stomping student[34]), insider dealing will alienate investors and potential investors, with adverse consequences for society as a whole. Most people would agree that stock markets, whether of the traditional or electronic variety, are efficient in allocating capital. For such markets to operate effectively and without inhibition, they require confidence and respect from their own societies and, increasingly, from the international community.

In the Second Reading of the Criminal Justice Bill, Earl Ferrers observed that, 'in order to operate successfully, those markets require investors to have confidence in their fairness. Insider dealing destroys that confidence'.[35] During discussion in the Committee Stage of the Companies Bill 1980, Mr Cecil Parkinson MP (then Secretary of State for Trade and Industry) stated that 'people who involve themselves in insider dealings are in the process of destroying confidence in the market'. Whilst other countries have played around with one or a mixture of the various theories, in the UK the justification for regulating insider abuse is based on the harm which it causes to investor confidence.

If it is felt that insider dealing is unfair and immoral, the economics, which are in any case equivocal, are not important and it is right and proper for those charged with protecting confidence in the integrity of the market to intervene. Neither is it important that scholars of jurisprudence and theologians might be minded to contend the illogicality of the common man's perception. At the end of the day, it is not scholars such as these (save for the few who have risen to become College bursars) who significantly influence the flow of funds directly to the stock market. As Professor Loss has observed, what is important in this context is the appearance of a concern to stamp out conduct which is considered abusive.[36] Of course, where action is taken which is neither effective nor credible, such intervention does nothing to foster confidence in the integrity of the market and may bring into disrepute those seeking to vindicate the markets and even the law.[37]

The significance of protecting the proper functioning of markets, whether in securities or other forms of property, has long been recognised and the law is considered a proper tool to achieve this. Indeed, the English common law, at a very early stage of its development, outlawed any practice or device which falsely enhanced the price of 'victuals' and other merchandise in the public markets, as being injurious to the public good.[38] The importance of protecting the market, rather than individuals within it, has been recognised in a number of cases[39] and, thus, to justify anti-insider dealing provisions on this basis underlines that it is the market and those depending upon the market who are harmed by such practices. This clearly shows that the notion that insider dealing is a victimless crime is a nonsense. Insofar as it undermines the proper functioning of the markets, it harms all those who have a direct or indirect interest in the efficiency of the markets – in other words, everyone. The British Government has traditionally sought to regulate insider dealing on the basis that it constitutes a wrong to the market and it is appropriate to utilise the criminal law to curb it. Whilst this approach may justify the intervention of legal rules, the appropriateness of which have long been recognised, it does not necessarily mean that the sledge-hammer of the criminal justice system is the most suitable instrument for surgery.[40]

NOTES

1   TC Newkirk *Recent SEC Enforcement Developments* (1991) 14th Corporate Crime Investigators Course, NSW.

2   The Insider Trading and Securities Fraud Enforcement Act 1988 amends the Securities Exchange Act 1934 by adding s 21A. Under s 21A(e), bounties are payable in the discretion of the SEC, to an amount up to 10 per cent of any civil penalty imposed by the SEC under s 21A. Bounties are not payable to 'officials' and would not, as a matter of policy, be paid to compliance officers.

3   *Company Investigations* HC 36 (1990).

4   See, for example, Psalm 38 'I was silent not opening my lips because this was all your doing'. See also M Ashe and Y Murphy *Insider Dealing* (Round Hall Press, 1992) at p 13.

5   *House of Commons Journals*, 25 November 1696.

6   An Act was passed in 1697 'To restrain the number and ill practice of brokers and stockjobbers'. See generally EV Morgan and WA Thomas *The Stock Exchange – Its History and Functions* (Elek Books, 1962) at Ch 1.

7   At the same time, Prime Minister Asquith listed six 'don'ts' for a minister, two of which forbade the use of 'official information . . . for his own private profit or that of his friends'. See R Brock 'Honest Graft' (1988) *London Review of Books*, June 23.

8   Prime Minister Edward Heath, on several occasions, referred to insider dealing as a wart on the face of capitalism and such comments were not uncommon in the debates on the Companies Bill 1973, which first sought to introduce specific provisions on insider dealing into English law.

9   Lord Lane CJ in *Attorney General's Reference (No 1 of 1988)* [1989] BCLC 193 at p 198.

10 For further discussion, see M Ashe and Y Murphy *Insider Dealing* (Round Hall Press, 1992) at Ch 2; B Rider *Insider Trading* (Jordans, 1983) at Ch 1; and B Rider and HL Ffrench *The Regulation of Insider Trading* (Macmillan, 1979) at Ch 1; and materials cited in these works.

11 See B Rider 'Insider Trading – A Crime of Our Time?' in *Current Legal Problems, Current Developments in Banking and Finance* (Stevens, 1989) at pp 63 et seq.

12 Whilst there is little evidence that Robert Maxwell engaged in insider dealing in the conventional sense, much of what he did, particularly towards the end of his Empire, was 'insider orientated'. See generally R Greenslade *Maxwell's Fall* (Simon & Schuster, 1992).

13 Whilst stock market surveillance has a relatively long history, its effectiveness in identifying cases of serious insider abuse is debatable.

14 *Insider Trading and the Stock Market* (The Free Press, 1966).

15 Ibid at p 14. The authors have declined to give the student a gender, being desirous not to offend anyone's sensibilities. Indeed, even in the chauvinistic days in which Professor Manne was writing, he carefully hides this piece of inside information (ibid at p 233, fn 42).

16   This is not a universal proposition, but is, in fact, rarely departed from. See generally Lord Goff and Gareth Jones *The Law of Restitution* (3rd edn) (Sweet & Maxwell).

17   In 'The Fiduciary Concept as applied to trading by corporate "insiders" in the United States' (1970) 33 MLR 34 at p 37. (Professor Loss, it will be noticed, was not so 'politically correct' on gender.)

18   See, for example, the arguments in *Diamond v Oreamuno* 24 NY 2d 494 (1969).

19   It has also been argued that insider self-interest distorts the efficiency and integrity of internal decision-making. See RJ Haft 'The effect of insider trading rules on the internal efficiency of the large corporation' (1982) 80 *Michigan Law Review* 1051.

20   See p 10 et seq.

21   See JC Shepherd *The Law of Fiduciaries* (Carswell, 1981) at Pt V; PD Finn *Equity and Commercial Relationships* (The Law Book Co, 1987) at Chs 6 and 7; and E McKendrick (Ed) *Commercial Aspects of Trusts and Fiduciary Obligations* (Oxford University Press, 1992) at Ch 7.

22   See p 40.

23   See p 66.

24   See p 68.

25   Although it has been suggested that this is the basis for the so-called 'misappropriation theory', which is not the ascendant approach to regulating insider abuse in the US, this is an over-simplistic view. The confidential information in question, which would be considered in the US as a species of property (see *US v Grossman* 843 F2d 78) must be misused in breach of a pre-existing fiduciary obligation. See *US v Carpenter* 791 F2d 1024 (2d Cir 1986), on appeal 484 US 19 (1987).

26   Whilst it seems to be the English law that a fiduciary cannot unilaterally impose an obligation of confidentiality on another, the position in the US is not as clear cut. In Britain, the obligation of a recipient of 'trust property' in such circumstances is not to further the breach of trust, see p 69.

27   This is very much the philosophy of the EC Directive on Insider Dealing, see p 14.

28   See DR Fischel 'Efficient Capital Markets, The Crash, and the Fraud on the Market Theory' (1989) 74 *Cornell Law Review* 907.

29   See, for example, the view of the US Supreme Court in *Laidlaw v Organ* 15 US (2 Wheat) 178 (1817) concerning the use of advanced knowledge in the tobacco market. Of course, Nathan Rothschild made considerable profits on the basis of the advance information which he obtained, largely through his own efforts and expense, on the outcome of the Battle of Waterloo.

30   See p 10 et seq.

31   See B Rider 'Insider Trading' in *Professional Responsibility* (Legal Research Foundation, 1987) at pp 73 et seq.

32   The main proponent of this view is Professor H Manne in *Insider Trading and the Stock Market* (The Free Press, 1966). The 'abstain or disclose' rule, developed by the US Courts in cases such as *SEC v Texas Gulf Sulphur Co* 401 F2d 88 (2d Cir 1968), has long been rejected on the basis that it inhibits the flow of information into the market. See *Dirks v SEC* 463 US 646 (1983). J Dennert *Insider Trading and the Cost of Capital in a Multi-period Economy* (1992) LSE Financial Markets Group Discussion Paper No 128 also criticises the operation of this rule on the basis that it inhibits liquidity.

33   See n 10 above and B Rider and HL Ffrench 'Should Insider Trading be Regulated? Some Initial Considerations' (1978) 95 SALJ 79.

34   See n 14 above.

35   Parliamentary Debates, House of Lords, 3 November 1992, col 1352.

36   'The Fiduciary Concept as applied to trading by corporate "insiders" in the United States' (1970) 33 MLR 34.

37   See B Rider 'Policing the City – Combating Fraud and Other Abuses in the Corporate Securities Industry' (1988) 41 *Current Legal Problems* 47; and B Rider 'Policing Insider

Dealing in Britain' in K Hopt and E Wymeersch (eds) *European Insider Dealing* (Butterworths, 1991) at Ch 17.

38 See B Rider, C Abrams and E Ferran *CCH Guide to the Financial Services Act 1986* (2nd edn)
(CCH) at Ch 1.

39 See Lord Ellenborough CH in *Rex v de Berenger* (1814) 105 ER 536 at p 538.

40 See M Ashe and L Counsell *Insider Trading* (Fourmat, 1990) at p 189.

DISCLOSURE

Insider dealing, as we have seen,[1] is all about taking advantage of information which has not yet been effectively discounted by the market or, in direct personal transactions, by the person with whom the insider is dealing. If price-sensitive information which is withheld from the market is kept to a minimum, there will be less opportunity for those desirous of exploiting it.[2] Mention has already been made of the likelihood that insiders will attempt to manipulate events so as to avoid prompt disclosure of information which they can exploit for their own ends.[3] This is a particular problem in situations where those in a position to influence the management of a company are also substantially interested in its securities. Thus, in many developing countries it is far more common to encounter insider manipulation of information than insiders merely attempting to beat the market. If it is important to encourage as much relevant information into the market as possible to facilitate sensible investment decisions, it makes sense to require issuers to disclose, through appropriate procedures, all information which might be reasonably considered to have an impact on the price of their securities.

A company will encounter disclosure obligations at various stages of its life. When it seeks to raise capital there are certain disclosure obligations tailored to the promotion of the securities. There are also continuous disclosure obligations designed to provide all those dealing with the company with adequate information to reach sensible decisions on the terms and circumstances of their relationship. Both promotional and continuous disclosure rely significantly on the medium of financial statements which, even if accurate and comprehensive, are inherently historic in perspective. Therefore, timely disclosure is probably of greater interest to the financial markets. This involves the immediate release of information in a readily understood form to the market, and is the most efficient means of disclosure in regard to significant and unexpected events.[4]

Promotional and continuous disclosure are governed by the requirements of company law[5] and, in the case of listed securities, the exacting requirements of The Stock Exchange.[6] Timely disclosure in Britain, unlike many other countries is, however, still primarily a stock exchange requirement, although there are specific obligations to disclose information on a timely basis in, for example, the *City Code on Takeovers and Mergers*. The Stock Exchange requires, as a condition of admission, that issuers disclose 'any information necessary to enable holders of the company's listed securities and the public to appraise the position of the company and to avoid the creation of a false market in its listed securities',[7] in addition to a series of specifically identified matters. The Stock Exchange has procedures for the announcement of such information which is designed to facilitate prompt and effective dissemination.[8] It also monitors compliance with this obligation as part of its ordinary market surveillance operation. It has been questioned, however, whether leaving this important obligation on issuers to *The Listing Rules* and not imposing a statutory obligation on those responsible for the management of the company to ensure proper adherence to The Stock Exchange's timely disclosure policy, is enough, both in terms of common sense or in relation to obligations under European Community law.[9]

The European Communities' Directive on the admission of securities to official listing on a stock exchange[10] provides that a company, which has been admitted to listing, must inform the public as soon as possible of any major new developments in its sphere of activity which are not public knowledge and which may, by virtue of their effect on its assets and liabilities or financial position or on the general course of its business lead to a substantial movement in the price of its shares. It is also provided that the relevant authorities responsible for the market may exempt an issuer from this obligation if the disclosure of a particular item of information would prejudice the legitimate interests of the company. Section 153(1) of the Financial Services Act 1986 seeks to implement these provisions by empowering The Stock Exchange to require, in its Listing Rules, such an obligation. Article 7 of the Insider Dealing Directive requires that the obligation to make prompt disclosure of material events in the Admissions Directive should be applied in regard to securities which although not officially listed are admitted to trading on a regulated market. The Treasury has published proposals for achieving this,[11] in the form of a draft regulation under the European Communities Act 1992. It is proposed to extend the present, hybrid rules of an essentially contractual nature, to issuers whose securities are traded on a market, the authorities of which have taken a view on the merits of the relevant security. Thus, the obligation to make prompt disclosure will apply to securities which are officially listed by the Stock Exchange or are traded on the Unlisted Securities Market – for the time being, but will not extend to issuers whose securities are traded on SEAQ International. Of course, issuers that are already officially listed are bound to make proper and timely disclosure under the present Listing Rules. The draft regulations, however, seek to impose a 'public law' duty on all relevant issuers to make timely disclosure. It is also provided that the rules of a recognised investment exchange must, at least, enable the exchange, in the event of a failure by an issuer to comply with its rules, to publish the fact that the issuer is in breach of its obligations and to proceed to publish the information itself. Whilst the imposition of such an obligation on issuers is to be welcomed, it remains to be seen whether the 'penalties' contemplated by the Treasury are sufficient, in the words of Art 13 of the Insider Dealing Directive, 'to promote compliance'. Perhaps specific criminal law penalties, as in certain other jurisdictions, would be a desirable addition.

Another important role that disclosure has in regulating insider abuse is in the obligations that are placed upon certain insiders to report promptly dealings which may give grounds for suspicion. Thus, since the Companies Act 1948, considerable reliance has been placed on the statutory obligation which is imposed on directors to report to their companies their own interests in the securities of the company as well as the interests of their spouses and children, as a means of discouraging insider trading.[12] There are other disclosure and reporting requirements in the *City Code on Takeovers and Mergers*[13] and in *The Listing Rules* of The Stock Exchange. To what extent insider abuse is discouraged by such obligations to report dealings is not clear. In practice, it is possible to evade such provisions through the use of nominees and associates, and criminal prosecutions for non-compliance are very rare.

NOTES

1   See p 3 et seq.
2   See B Rider 'Insider Trading – A Question of Confidence' (1980) *LS Gaz* 113; P Fenn, Al McGuire and D Prentice 'Information Imbalances and the Securities Markets' in K Hopt and E Wymeersch (eds) *European Insider Dealing* (Butterworths, 1990) at Ch 1.
3   See p 4.
4   See generally B Rider and HL Ffrench *The Regulation of Insider Trading* (Macmillan, 1979) at Ch 4 for the development of timely disclosure policies.
5   See *Gore-Browne on Companies* (44th edn) (Jordans) at Chs 10 and 22.
6   ('The Yellow Book') at Chs 8 and 9.
7   Ibid at Ch 9.1. Reference should also be made to the *Model Code* see App 3; and see generally B Hanigan *Insider Dealing* (Kluwer, 1988) at pp 55 et seq.
8   See p 34.
9   See generally JH Dalhuisen *The New UK Securities Legislation and the EC 1992 Program* (North Holland, 1989) at Ch 4.
10 EC Directive No 79/279, Sch C5(9).
11 *Implementation of Article 7 of The Insider Dealing Directive* (HM Treasury, 1993).
12 See the Companies Act 1985, s 324 to 328 and Sch 13, Pts I and IV; and note s 235 in regard to disclosure in the annual report.
13 See the *City Code on Takeovers and Mergers* at Rules 8, 24.3 and 25.3.

THE LEGISLATIVE BACKGROUND

Following a number of unsuccessful attempts to enact specific provisions rendering insider trading a criminal offence,[1] Part V of the Companies Act 1980 achieved this. The relevant provisions were re-enacted, with minor amendments, in the Company Securities (Insider Dealing) Act 1985. Whilst many of the concepts in that Act are found in the CJA 1993, there are a number of very significant differences. Indeed, to a large degree the present law reflects a different philosophy from the earlier enactments. Whilst the importance of maintaining confidence in the integrity of the market remains central, there is a manifest break with the tradition of regarding insider abuse as essentially a breach of attenuated fiduciary relationship. Thus, as we shall see, under the new law it is not necessary for the insider to be connected with either the source of the relevant information or the issuer of the securities in question; nor is it necessary for the information to be confidential in the traditional sense of that word. Such notions reflect the company law perspective and are, thus, more orientated to notions associated with breach of directors' duties, than market fairness and equality of information.[2] The earlier UK legislation was, insofar as it strove to vindicate the integrity of the market, a curious mixture of what might be described as the 'stewardship' and 'market fraud' approaches.

The change in form and substance of UK law is a direct result of the harmonisation of company law within the European Community. Whilst in more recent years the debate on regulation of such abuses as insider dealing and market manipulation has tended to emphasise the importance of fostering a sound and respected capital market, there is no doubt that the initiative in seeking to impose standard or equivalent regulations arose directly from the company law programme.[3] However, the first reference which the authors have found to insider dealing regulation in the context of the European Community is in the report of a Committee of Experts,[4] appointed by the European Commission, to consider how best to facilitate the development of an effective and efficient European capital market. In this report the Committee of Experts emphasised the importance of investors having 'at their disposal sufficient and reasonably homogenous information on securities dealt in other markets'. Whilst the facilitation of market development was clearly recognised to be of critical importance in furthering the objectives of the Community, the institutions of the Community, until recently, attempted to deal with insider abuse primarily through the harmonisation of company law. A working party was set up as early as 1976[5] and there had been ad hoc deliberations and studies prior to this. Indeed, it was not until 1983[6] that the European Commission finally resolved that it would be appropriate to regulate insider abuse through an EC Directive on Insider Dealing rather than merely a recommendation. The text of the 'initial' final Directive was very different from the earlier discussion documents and bore a marked difference from the version which the Council finally accepted.[7] As a result it is rather simplistic to attempt to discern an underlying philosophy other than pragmatism; although from the Preamble to the Directive,[8] it is clear that the concept of market egalitarianism remains a guiding principle. The Directive also states that 'for the market to be able to play its role effectively, every measure should be taken to ensure that the market operates smoothly'. The Directive observes that the 'smooth operation of the market depends to a large extent on the confidence it inspires in investors'. For such confidence, the Directive states that investors must be assured that they are 'on an equal footing' and will be protected against the improper use of inside information. Thus, according to the European Commission, 'by benefiting certain investors as compared with others, insider dealing is likely to undermine this confidence and may therefore prejudice the smooth operation of the market'. Even if it can be accepted that it is desirable economically, socially and politically to have smooth markets, whatever that may mean, it is highly debatable whether insider dealing is likely to ruffle markets. Indeed, as we have seen[9] there are arguments to the effect that insider dealing actually encourages information into the market. Furthermore, it may be questioned whether the average investor actually wants, let alone expects, to be on an equal footing in any respect, let alone in regard to the availability of information.[10] Insofar as it is possible to distil, other than in an anecdotal sense, investor motivation, it would seem that most decisions will, at least in part, be influenced by a view that one person is better informed or at least a little more perceptive than the majority. It seems unusual that Europe has now espoused the philosophy of equal access to information when, after almost half a century of experience it has been rejected in the US as not being a sensible basis for regulating insider abuse.[11]

Whilst the Directive does talk about 'taking advantage of inside information', the fundamental conflict between encouraging, through diligence and perceptive analysis, better investment decisions on the one hand, and the exploitation of privileged information acquired through no merit but chance or position on the other, is addressed merely in terms of assertion rather than convincing analysis. No matter how sympathetic the authors may be to the objectives of the European Community, they cannot help but feel that things would have been better left as they were before the Directive. There are differences of emphasis and, in certain respects, of substance between what is prescribed in the Directive and what the UK Parliament (after due deliberation albeit without much consultation) has enacted.[12] Whether these 'differences' will give rise to problems remains to be seen. The temptation to pursue such issues is great, particularly in the context of a criminal prosecution.

Where UK law is more strict than the law under the Directive[13] it is hard to contemplate a viable complaint on the part of a defendant unless there is an issue of Constitutional significance or, possibly, one relating to human rights. It would be unusual for a defendant in a criminal case to contend that UK law is over-lax unless it brought into issue the interpretation or certainty of a specific offence. What is more conceivable, however, is that a litigant may seek to argue that the Directive, insofar as it is directly applicable, fosters a civil claim against an insider. Such an argument may be made on, for example, the contention that s 57(2) of CJA 1993 which sets out when information is made public, is more restrictive than the Directive. The Preamble to the Directive and the Directive's legislative history indicate the desirability of a period for dissemination. Whilst it would seem that such an argument could not justify the implication of a specific obligation upon another individual[14] (in this case the insider) it appears that UK courts would be bound to interpret and apply UK law so as to give proper effect to the Directive.[15] Whilst this may constitute a fertile ground for academic analysis, the authors are sceptical as to the practical implications for investors, let alone insiders.

A more likely scenario may be an action against the British Government for failure to adequately implement the Directive. In *Francovich v Republic of Italy*[16] the European Court of Justice accepted that the EEC Treaty created a legal order which is binding upon member states and citizens and which gives rights to, and imposes obligations, on citizens. The European Court of Justice considered that it was important that individuals who suffer loss as a result of a failure of a Member State's breach of European Community law should have a cause of action for compensation against the state in question. It would seem that the scope of the CJA 1993 is narrower than the Directive in regard to the definition of inside information. The UK Government has excluded from the offences the use of information which has a general impact, such as information relating to a change of Government policy, which could have a significant impact on the market and the price of a given security.[17] It is conceivable, given the worthy statements in the Directive's Preamble and its legislative history emphasising the importance of protecting investors, that an investor who can establish loss as a result of this 'failure' to implement the Directive in what might be considered a significant respect, could seek compensation.

The Directive is not the only step which the European Commission has taken in fighting insider dealing. In 1977, the European Commission promulgated a Recommendation,[18] constituting a code of conduct for dealings in securities which specifically prohibits insider abuse. The Recommendation, however, does not give rise to any legal consequences and is little more than a standard for countries to contemplate when preparing their own regulations. In practical terms, it has had minimal effect in the UK. There have also been various initiatives in relation to the European Company Statute[19] and the duties of directors and officers of companies.[20] There are also provisions in other Directives relating to takeovers and corporate disclosure which are relevant.[21] Perhaps the most important is the provision in the Directive on admission of securities to Official Listing,[22] which places on such issuers an obligation to inform the public as soon as possible

> 'of any major new developments in its sphere of activity which are not public knowledge and which may, by virtue of their effect on its assets and liabilities or financial position or on the general course of its business, lead to substantial movements in the prices of its shares'.

Whilst timely disclosure is required as a condition for admission to The Stock Exchange in the UK, it is not yet a legislative requirement.[23] Earlier drafts of the Insider Dealing Directive contained provisions relating to timely disclosure,[24] but these were dropped in the final draft.

NOTES

1　See generally B Rider and HL Ffrench *The Regulation of Insider Trading* (Macmillan, 1979) at Ch 6.

2　See PL Davies 'The European Community's Directive on Insider Dealing: From Company Law to Securities Markets Regulation?' (1991) 11 *Oxford Journal of Legal Studies* 92.

3　See B Rider and HL Ffrench *The Regulation of Insider Trading* (above) at pp 263 et seq.

4　*The Development of a European Capital Market* (Commission of the European Communities, 1966); this report is commonly known as the *Segre Report* after the name of the Committee's Chairman.

5　See *Working Paper* XV/140/76-M, 18 May 1976 and, in particular, *Working Paper No 1 Coordination of the Rules and Regulations Governing Insider Trading* XV/206/76, 9 August 1976.

6　See *Working Paper No 6* XV/79/83-EN, 17 March 1983.

7　See T Tridimas 'Insider Trading: European Harmonisation and National Law Reform' (1991) 40 ICLQ 919 at p 920.

8　Council Directive coordinating regulations on insider dealing (89/592/EEC).

9　See p 3 et seq.

10　See A Alcock 'In defence of insider dealing' (1990) NLJ 1470.

11　See *Chiarella v US* 445 US 222 (1980) and *Dirks v SEC* 436 US 646 (1983).

12　There has been considerable criticism of the Government's limited and selective consultation on the legislative proposals. Apart from the DTI's preliminary Consultative Document which was published in 1990 and some notes published at the time that the Criminal Justice Bill was introduced, virtually no public consultation occurred. For criticism of the Government's handling of this legislation, see, for example, Lord Alexander, House of Lords, 3 November 1992, at p 1363. It appears that there was little meaningful discussion with the professional groups, other than on a highly selective basis. See B Knight (1992) *The Lawyer*, September 29, at p 5.

13 Article 6 of the Directive permits 'more stringent' provisions to be added by Member States.

14 See *Marleasing SA v La Commercial International de Alimentacion SA* [1992] 1 CMLR 305.

15 See cases at n 14 above and *Von Colson v Land Nordrhein Westfahlen* (1984) ECR 1891 and, in particular, *Litster v Forth Dry Dock and Engineering Co Ltd* [1990] AC 546 and *Pepper v Hart* [1993] 1 All ER 42.

16 *Francovich v Republic of Italy* and *Bonifaci v Republic of Italy* (joined cases) C6/90 and C9/90 (1991) November 19.

17 See p 32.

18 Commission Recommendation of 25 July 1977 concerning a European Code of Conduct relating to transactions in transferable securities (77/534/EEC) (OJ 1977 No L 212/37).

19 See generally B Rider and M Ashe 'The Insider Dealing Directive' in M Andenas and S Kenyon-Slade (eds) *EC Financial Market Regulation and Company Law* (Sweet & Maxwell, 1993) at Ch 12.

20 See n 17 above. The provisions on insider dealing which were previously in the Draft Fifth Directive on the structure and management of public companies have been dropped as it was thought preferable to deal with insider abuse in a specific measure.

21 See generally n 17 above and K Hopt and E Wymeersch (eds) *European Insider Dealing* (Butterworths, 1990) at Chs 5 and 6.

22 Council Directive co-ordinating the conditions for the admission of securities to official stock exchange listing (79/279/EEC) at Sch C, para 5(a).

23 But see p 10.

24 See Proposal for a Council Directive co-ordinating regulations on insider trading Com (87) 111 Final, 21 May 1987, Art 7. The DTI in its Consultative Document *The Law on Insider Dealing* (1990) at para A.2 expressed the view that this would be better applied through secondary rather than primary legislation. This is what the Treasury Consultation Document entitled *Implementation of Article 7 of the Insider Dealing Directive* (1993) proposes.

PART 2

THE LEGISLATION ANALYSED

INTRODUCTION

There were three attempts to introduce legislation outlawing insider dealing during the 1970s. During the passage of the Companies Bill 1980, which for the first time included provisions specifically directed at insider dealing, the Government was criticised for introducing a large number of amendments at a relatively late stage. In regard to the Criminal Justice Act 1993 (CJA 1993), the Government has again been widely criticised for a manifest lack of adequate consultation with other than a very select circle[1] and also for virtually rewriting the provisions during the passage of the Criminal Justice Bill through the House of Commons (over six months after the Bill had been introduced in the House of Lords). The last-minute amendments were a pity since the consultation process had started early in the sense that a consultative document had been produced by the Department of Trade and Industry in 1989 (although draft clauses of the legislation were only circulated by the Treasury among the select few in the summer preceding the introduction of the Bill in the autumn of 1992). In the result, Part V of the CJA 1993 bears little resemblance to the Bill which was introduced into the House of Lords.

NOTES

1   Parliamentary Debates, House of Lords, 3 Nov 1992, col 1365 (Lord Alexander of Weedon)

GENERAL CRIMINAL OFFENCES

The general criminal law has always been concerned to protect the integrity of public markets.[1] Indeed, there are a number of ancient offences outlawing interference with the proper operation of markets in the early criminal law, which were, for a time, also rendered crimes under statutes.[2] Today, however, most of these offences would be covered by s 47 of the Financial Services Act 1986 (FSA 1986), which deals with false statements, manipulative practices[3] and the crime of conspiracy to defraud. In practice, the more general offences relating to interference with the market would not be relevant in cases of simple insider dealing, unless, of course, there has been manipulation and fraudulent conduct.

Section 323 of the Companies Act 1985[4] makes it an offence for a director to buy a put or call option in the securities of his company, its holding, subsidiary or sister company, provided that the relevant security is listed on The Stock Exchange. This prohibition also extends to the director's spouse and infant children. It should be noted that this provision is a complete prohibition on the purchase of such options, whether the insider has inside information or not.

It is doubtful whether the English law would regard the misappropriation of inside information as capable of amounting to theft of property under the Theft Act 1968. Indeed, unlike in certain other jurisdictions, the weight of authority is against information being considered property for the purposes of the criminal law.[5] It is also doubtful whether a charge could be brought under s 47(1) of the FSA 1986[6] where an insider deliberately conceals material insider information for the purpose of inducing an investment transaction. The general rule under English law is that there is no obligation on a person in possession of superior information, even if it is obtained from a privileged source or by virtue of a privileged position, to disclose it to another, even though he appreciates that if that other had access to the relevant information he would not deal on the terms which he does.[7] In other words, mere silence, and even concealment, in the absence of a specific duty to disclose, cannot amount to fraud. It has also been argued that it cannot be dishonest not to disclose information in regard to which the insider may be under a duty to keep confidential.[8] It would, therefore, seem that s 47(1) of the FSA 1986 will be relevant to cases of insider trading only when the insider is under an independent legal duty to disclose the relevant information.

NOTES

1   See *Russell on Crime* (12 edn) (Stevens) at Ch 100.

2   51 Hen 3, st 6: 5 & 6 Edw 6, c 14. See also, in regard to the civil law relating to disturbance, JG Pease (1916) LQR 199.
3   See generally B Rider, C Abrams and E Ferran *CCH Guide to the Financial Services Act 1986* (2nd edn) (CCH) at pp 127 et seq; and A Arlidge and J Parry *Fraud* (Waterlow, 1985) at pp 215 et seq.
4   This provision was originally introduced in the Companies Act 1967, on the recommendation of the Company Law Committee (1962) (Cmnd 1749) at para 90.
5   See p 69.
6   See n 3 above.
7   See p 63.
8   See p 62 at n 5.

THE OFFENCE OF INSIDER DEALING

The CJA 1993 received Royal Assent on 27 July 1993 and is expected, in relation to its provisions on insider dealing, to be brought into force towards the end of 1993. It will replace the Company Securities (Insider Dealing) Act 1985 and will represent an extension of the basis of liability for the insider dealing offence. The CJA 1993 contains a wider definition of 'securities' and 'insider' and the nature of inside information has been altered.

The insider dealing offence created by Part V of the CJA 1993 is aimed at individuals engaging in three classes of conduct in particular circumstances which are:

(a) dealing in price-affected securities on the basis of inside information;[1]
(b) encouraging another person to do so;[2] and
(c) disclosing inside information.[3]

The circumstances in which the first two offences may be committed are:[4]

(a) by dealing in securities on a regulated market;[5] or
(b) where the person dealing in the price-affected securities relies on a professional intermediary or is himself acting as a professional intermediary.[6]

The legislation is aimed at insider dealing based in the UK[7] but the offence cannot be applied to anything done by an individual acting on behalf of a public sector body in pursuit of monetary policies, policies with respect to exchange rates or the management of either public debt or foreign exchange reserves.[8] This exclusion exists principally to remove from the scope of the legislation the activities of the Government in managing the economy. However, while it applies to Government activities in relation to economic management it would not, for example, apply to a Government sale of shares.

A series of defences is provided by the legislation to deal with, what may broadly be described as, motive[9] and also with particular market situations.[10] These are designed with the object of trying to ensure that certain innocent transactions and bona fide market practices are not inhibited by the laws curbing insider dealing.

A prosecution in England and Wales or in Northern Ireland may be instituted only with the consent of the Secretary of State or Director of Public Prosecutions.[11] In Scotland, all prosecutions are instituted by the Lord Advocate.

If an individual is convicted of insider dealing after summary trial, he is liable to a fine not exceeding the statutory maximum, currently £5,000,[12] or a term of imprisonment not exceeding six months, or both.[13] If convicted on indictment, there is no maximum limit on the fine and the term of imprisonment may be up to seven years.[14] As is the case with summary convictions, both a fine and a custodial sentence may be imposed after conviction on indictment. However, no contract is void or unenforceable by reason only of a breach of the insider dealing prohibition.[15]

NOTES

1   CJA 1993, s 52(1). 'Dealing' is defined by CJA 1993, s 55. See p 48. For the securities covered, see CJA 1993, s 54(1) and p 24 below. Price-affected securities are defined by CJA 1993, s 56(2). See p 24.

2   CJA 1993, s 52(2)(a).

3   Ibid, s 52(2)(b).

4   Ibid, s 52(3). For the territorial scope of the offence, see ibid, s 62 and p 59.

5   Defined by CJA 1993, s 60(1). See p 25.

6   Defined by CJA 1993, s 59. See p 28.

7   CJA 1993, s 79(2). For the territorial scope of the offence, see ibid, s 62 and p 59.

8   CJA 1993, s 63(1).

9   Ibid, s 53. See p 54.

10   CJA 1993, Sch 1. See p 56.

11   CJA 1993, s 61(2) and (3).

12   Magistrates' Courts Act 1980, s 32 and CJA 1991, s 17(2)(c).

13   CJA 1993, s 61(1)(a).

14   Ibid, s 61(1)(b).

15   Ibid, s 63(2). See *Chase Manhattan Equities Ltd v Goodman* [1991] BCLC 897 for an example of a contract held unenforceable for breach of the Company Securities (Insider Dealing) Act 1985, notwithstanding s 8(3) of that Act, which was a similar provision but provided that no contract was to be 'void or voidable' by reason of a breach of the insider dealing prohibition.

SECURITIES COVERED BY THE OFFENCE

The list of securities to which the insider dealing legislation applies[1] closely mirrors the list of investments within the scope of the Financial Services Act 1986 (FSA 1986)[2] and marks a broadening of the scope of the insider dealing offence representing the enactment of a Government policy of long standing.[3] The list of securities also conforms with the approach of the EC Directive on Insider Dealing,[4] so that not only corporate securities and instruments based on such securities are included but also gilts, local authority stock and instruments derived from corporate securities.

However, the object is not to catch all transactions in these securities in all circumstances, since the purpose of the legislation is to ensure confidence in the market in its broadest sense.[5] Accordingly, the circumstances in which the insider dealing prohibitions apply are limited to situations where there is a ready trade in those securities.

The legislation attempts to do this by the following means:

(a) it defines the securities which it covers;[6]
(b) it defines the conditions applicable which bring those securities within its parameters;[7] and
(c) it sets out the circumstances of dealing in those securities with which it is concerned.[8]

The securities presently covered are set out in the CJA 1993[9] and are as follows (but there is a power to amend that list of securities by Order).[10]

1   Shares and stock in the share capital of a company ('shares').

2   Any instrument creating or acknowledging indebtedness which is issued by a company or public sector body, including, in particular, debentures, debenture stock, loan stock, bonds and certificates of deposit ('debt securities').

3   Any right (whether conferred by warrant or otherwise) to subscribe for shares or debt securities ('warrants').

4   The rights under any depositary receipt; a 'depositary receipt' being a certificate or other record whether or not in the form of a document, which is issued by or on behalf of a person who holds any shares, debt securities or warrants of a particular issuer and which acknowledges that another person is entitled to rights in relation to those securities or securities of the same kind.[11]

5   Any option to acquire or dispose of shares, debt securities, warrants, depositary receipts, futures or contracts for differences.

6   Rights under a contract for the acquisition or disposal of shares, debt securities, warrants, depositary receipts, options or contracts for differences under which delivery is to be made at a future date and at a price agreed when the contract is made or at a date and price determined in accordance with the contract.[12]

7   Rights under a contract which does not provide for the delivery of securities but whose purpose or pretended purpose is to secure a profit or avoid a loss by reference to fluctuations in a share index or similar factor connected with securities or the price of particular securities or the interest rate offered on money placed on deposit.[13]

The circumstances, when dealing in these securities, which may bring an individual within the scope of the insider dealing offence[14] are that the deal occurs on a regulated market or that the person dealing either relies on, or is himself acting as, a professional intermediary.[15]

What is or is not a regulated market will be specified by statutory instrument.[16] At the time of writing, no statutory instrument had been made but a draft statutory instrument was available. The regulated markets specified in that draft include those which are recognised stock exchanges under the previous insider dealing legislation,[17] namely The International Stock Exchange of the United Kingdom and the Republic of Ireland Limited, the National Association of Securities Dealers Automated Quotations System (NASDAQ) and the Swedish Options Market (OM (London)).

In addition, given a wider definition of 'securities',[18] there is included The London International Financial Futures Exchange (Administration). Also included in the draft statutory instrument are the major exchanges in the Member States of the European Community. Accordingly, the stock exchanges in, for example, Athens, Brussels, Frankfurt, Hanover, Lisbon, Luxembourg, Madrid, Milan, Norway, Oporto, Paris, Rome and Venice will be among those regarded as regulated markets.[19]

Finally, other markets which meet criteria specified in the draft statutory instrument will also be regulated markets. The criteria proposed at the time of writing are that:

(a)   the head office of the investment exchange under the rules of which the market are established is situated in a Member State of the European Community; and

(b)   the market is subject in the Member State in which that head office is situated as to:

(i)   the manner in which it operates;
(ii)   the means by which access may be had to the facilities it provides;
(iii) the conditions to be satisfied before a security may be dealt in by means of, or before its price may be quoted on, its facilities; and

(iv) the reporting and publication of dealing effected by means of its facilities.

Subject, therefore, to the territorial scope[19] of the offence, insider deals on the above markets or in reliance on or by a professional intermediary in the defined securities if they are price affected and fall within the scope of certain conditions,[20] will be covered by the insider dealing legislation. These conditions are as follows.

1   In relation to any security, it must be dealt in or under the rules of, or have its price quoted on, a regulated market.

2   In relation to a warrant, the rights to subscribe must be for any shares or debt security dealt in or under the rules of, or have their price quoted on, a regulated market.

3   In relation to a depositary receipt, the rights under it must be in respect of any share or debt security dealt in or under the rules of, or have their price quoted on, a regulated market.

4   In relation to an option or a future, that the options or rights under it are in respect of any share, debt security or depositary receipt which is dealt in or under the rules of, or have their price quoted on, a regulated market or in respect of a depositary receipt the rights under which are in any share or debt security so dealt in or has its price so quoted.

5   In relation to a contract for differences,[21] that the purpose or pretended purpose of a contract for differences is to secure a profit or avoid a loss by reference to fluctuation, either in the price of any shares or debt securities or depositary receipt which are dealt in on or under the rules of, or have their price quoted as a regulated market or any depositary receipt in respect of such share or debt security.

NOTES

1   CJA 1993, Sch 2.
2   FSA 1986, Sch 1. Under s 12 of the Company Securities (Insider Dealing) Act 1985 the definition of securities was confined to corporate securities and certain of their derivatives.
3   See the White Paper *Financial Services in the United Kingdom* (Cmnd 9472).
4   Council Directive (89/592/EEC), Art 1(2).
5   Parliamentary Debates, House of Commons, Standing Committee B, 10 June 1993, col 164 (per the Economic Secretary).
6   CJA 1993, s 54(1) and Sch 2.
7   Ibid, s 54(2). At the time of writing, only the draft statutory instrument was available as the CJA 1993 had not been brought into force.

8   Ibid, s 52(3).
9   Ibid, Sch 2.
10 Ibid, s 54(2).
11 Ibid, Sch 2, para 4(2).
12 Ibid, Sch 2, para 6(2)(a).
13 In *City Index v Leslie* [1992] 1 QB 98 (CA) the comparable, although slightly different, wording in Sch 1, para 9 to the FSA 1986 was considered to include not only hedging transactions but also naked bets.
14 CJA 1993, s 52(1) and (2).
15 CJA 1993, s 52(3).
16 Ibid, s 60(1).
17 Company Securities (Insider Dealing Act) 1985, s 16(1). Insider Dealing (Recognised Stock Exchange) Order 1989, SI 1989/2165; Insider Dealing (Recognised Stock Exchange) (No 2) Order 1990, SI 1990/47.
18 See n 17 above.
19 A full list of proposed regulated markets appears in Appendix 2. For the territorial extent of the offence see CJA 1993, s 62 and p 59.
20 To be specified by statutory instrument. At the time of writing, only the draft statutory instrument was available (Insider Dealing (Regulated Markets and Securities) Order 1993, see App 1).
21 For an example of a contract for differences related to an index, see *City Index v Leslie* [1992] 1 QB 98(CA).

THE RELEVANT DEALS IN SECURITIES

A deal in securities is essential to the dealing offence but is also of relevance to the encouragement offence insofar as the encouragement has to be targeted at a dealing. While not of direct relevance to the form of the disclosure offence, a defence is available where no dealing was expected.[1] The type of deal with which the CJA 1993 is concerned is limited.[1]

If deals in securities do not occur on a regulated market they will only be within the insider dealing legislation if the person dealing relies on a professional intermediary or is himself a professional intermediary.[2]

A person will rely on a professional intermediary only if the professional intermediary either acquires or disposes of securities (whether as principal or agent) in relation to the dealing or acts as intermediary between persons taking part in the dealing.[3] If, therefore, the securities dealt in fall within the categories above, the insider dealing offence will be relevant unless the transaction is truly a private deal off the market without the intervention of a market professional.

A professional intermediary is defined by the CJA 1993 as a person who carries on a business of acquiring or disposing of securities (whether as principal or agent) or a business of acting as an intermediary between persons taking part in any dealing in securities.[4] Individuals employed by such a person to carry out these activities are also treated as professional intermediaries.[5] A person will not be treated as a professional intermediary if these activities are merely incidental to other activities or if he only occasionally conducts one of those activities.[6]

NOTES

1   See p 55.
2   CJA 1993, s 52(3).
3   Ibid, s 59(4).
4   Ibid, s 59(1)(a).
5   Ibid, s 59(1)(b).
6   Ibid, s 58(3).

INSIDE INFORMATION

Nature of inside information under the new and old law

Probably the most crucial and difficult issue in insider dealing law is the nature of inside information. Each of the three offences provided for in the CJA 1993 requires inside information as an essential element but, even with the benefit of definition, inside information remains a rarefied concept. At any one time a substantial amount of information will flow through a company and be in the possession of its directors, employees and advisers. Some of this will be confidential and may, if it were made public, have some slight impact on share prices. The object of insider dealing law is not to be concerned with this sort of information but, in the words of one celebrated US case,[1] it should deal with:

'situations which are essentially extraordinary in nature and which are reasonably certain to have a substantial effect on the market price of the security'.

Thus, for example, during the Committee Stage of the previous insider dealing legislation in 1979, the Minister emphasised that 'the kind of knowledge we are after is knowledge of dramatic events, major happenings, and things which will transform the Company's prospects'.[2] The CJA 1993 tests the quality of information to determine whether it is inside information by reference to whether or not it has a 'significant' effect on price.

Under the CJA 1993, inside information has four characteristics.[3] It is information which:

(a) relates to particular securities or to a particular issuer of securities or particular issuers of securities and not to securities generally or to issuers of securities generally;
(b) is specific or precise;
(c) has not been made public; and
(d) if it were made public would be likely to have a significant effect on the price of any securities.

In previous legislation,[4] inside information was referred to as 'unpublished price-sensitive information' and had the following elements.

1 The information had to relate to specific matters relating or of concern (directly or indirectly) to the company whose securities were dealt in, which was not of a general nature relating, or of concern, to the company.

2   The information was not to be generally known to those persons
    accustomed or likely to deal in the company's securities.

3   The information had to be likely materially to affect the price of the
    securities.

4   The information had to be such that it would be reasonable to expect a
    primary insider not to disclose it, except for the proper performance of
    his functions.

The aim of both definitions is basically the same – that is to cover
information which relates to a specific sector as well as to a specific security,
while excluding general information. The approach in the CJA 1993 is
based on that of the EC Directive on Insider Dealing[5] and it seems to
achieve that aim more clearly than its predecessor, which could be criticised on grounds of obscurity. However, the new approach is also wider in
its effect.

'Particular securities' and 'particular issuer(s) of securities'

The first characteristic of the definition of inside information in the CJA
1993 makes clear that information which relates to a specific sector is
included, as well as that which relates to a specific security. Accordingly,
information may still be inside information although it has nothing specifically to do with a particular company or its shares but rather to the industry
in which that company participates.

Information which relates to an issuer will include information which
comes from within the issuer. Thus, for example, information about a
substantial increase or cut in profits of a company, which clearly has its
source within the organisation, will certainly be information which relates
to an issuer. However, the information referred to in the CJA 1993 also
includes information arising outside the issuer. Perhaps a classic example
will be a takeover bid, where the proposal to acquire the company's shares
emanates from the bidder. Similarly, information relating to securities may
be internal, such as a dividend, but may be external, such as a decision
about the company's listing by The Stock Exchange.

These examples are straightforward but the question of when information relates to a particular security or particular issuer or issuers may not
necessarily be one that is simple. While it is clear that the definition does
not include information which relates to securities generally or to issuers
generally there is much information which, although not of that general
quality, is not related to a particular security but may, nonetheless, have a
significant effect on its price if made public.

If, for example, an employee of Airline A, in the course of his employment has confidential information about Airline A giving up two routes on

which the only competition is Airline B, this information is likely to be advantageous if he were to purchase shares in Airline B, before the information is published. Undoubtedly, the information has its most direct relationship with Airline A and, given that the employee has the information as an insider (and assuming it to be price sensitive, negatively, in relation to Airline A's shares) he should not deal in Airline A's shares by, for instance, selling them before the news reaches the public domain and their price drops. However, the information may also be said to relate to Airline B. It would be curious if the employee, who clearly has the information as an insider, were committing an offence by selling shares in Airline A and not committing an offence by purchasing shares in Airline B. In both cases he would have the same information as an insider and in both cases that information would have a significant effect on the prices of each share. Yet, without further clarification it could be argued that the information did not relate to Airline B but only related to Airline A. Such a result would, of course, offend common sense.

Further clarification is given in CJA 1993, s 59(4), which states:

> 'For the purposes of this Part, information shall be treated as relating to an issuer of securities which is a company not only where it is about the company but also where it may affect the company's business prospects.'

This provision appears to ensure that, in the example given above, the information relates not only to Airline A but to Airline B since it will affect Airline B's business prospects, ie by Airline A giving up two routes this will be beneficial to the business of Airline B.

The inclusion of 'business prospects' attracted some criticism in Parliament since it was said to make the definition of 'inside information' far too wide.

An explanation for this inclusion was given by the Earl of Caithness on behalf of HM Government in the debate on the Criminal Justice Bill in the House of Lords.[6] He said:

> 'It is included because the Government believe that it is essential our insider dealing legislation catch as inside information, information which, while not relating directly to a company, would nonetheless be likely to have a significant effect on the price of its shares. An example of information in this category might be important regulatory decisions and information about a company's major customer or supplier.'[7]

It is undoubtedly true that it is this broad-based approach to the definition of inside information, together with an expanded approach to who is an insider,[8] which has led to the widespread concern that the CJA 1993 is too wide in ambit. A simple comparison between the elements of the Company Securities (Insider Dealing) Act 1985 definition and the CJA 1993 definition shows the wider approach of the new legislation.

The exclusion from the definition of information which relates to securities generally, or to issuers of securities generally, appears to mean that, for example, confidential information of a particular Government economic policy which will impact on the market generally is outside the definition of inside information. In this respect the CJA 1993 appears to be less strict than the EC Directive on Insider Dealing, Art 1(1), which places no such restriction and specifically includes such general news. The Directive is, therefore, extremely far reaching.[9] The CJA 1993 clearly goes for a narrower approach and in this regard, at least, is consistent with the approach behind the Company Securities (Insider Dealing) Act 1985.

'Specific' and 'precise'

The second characteristic of inside information is that it must either be 'specific' or 'precise'. Information is precise when it is exact. The reason for putting in the word 'specific' was because, if left on its own, the word 'precise' might have the effect that, for example, information that there will be a huge dividend increase would not amount to inside information without also details of the quantum of the increase. The word 'specific' is intended to ensure that information about a huge dividend cut can be inside information, whilst mere rumour and untargeted information cannot.[10]

Arguably, the use of the word 'specific' may eliminate more than mere rumour and untargeted information. In one Australian case the phrase 'specific information' was held to denote 'not merely that it [the information] is precisely definable but that its entire content can be precisely and unequivocally expressed and discerned'.[11] This led the court to the conclusion that 'specific information' had to have an existence of its own, quite apart from the operation of any process of deduction.[12] On this approach the deduction that a company was prepared to purchase a large tranche of shares from several persons from the fact of knowledge of a purchase of shares from one person would not be specific information. While such a view has its attractions it is often inferences drawn from facts which affect market price and, theoretically, if the facts are not made public the insider who has them needs also to be restrained from trading on inferences made from those facts.

But whatever the correct approach to inferences may be, information may still be specific even though, as information, it has a vague quality. Thus, information that a company is having a financial crisis has been held to be specific.[13] Also, information as to the possibility of a takeover may be regarded as specific information[14] and will certainly rank as precise, given that it is more than mere rumour.

In the Standing Committee stage of the Criminal Justice Bill an Opposition amendment in the House of Commons, to the definition of the words 'specific' and 'precise', was rejected. However, some idea of what situations the Government considered those words would cover was given in the following examples.

EXAMPLE 1

An analyst had lunch with the chairman of a company and as they left the restaurant they saw his battered BMW in the car park. The analyst said to the chairman 'Isn't it time you got a new car?' The chairman replied that he would not be buying a new car that year. The Economic Secretary considered that these circumstances would lead neither to specific nor precise information in relation to the company, given that there could be many reasons for the statement, including the fact that the chairman may personally have been experiencing a hard time financially.[15]

EXAMPLE 2

If during the lunch, the chairman had said 'Our results will be much better than the market expects or knows', the Economic Secretary said that this would not be precise information because there was no disclosure of what the results of the company would be. However, it would, he said, be specific information because the chairman would have disclosed something about the company's results, whilst making it quite obvious that the information had not been made public.[16]

'Made public'

The third characteristic of inside information is that it has not been made public. In the original drafts of the Criminal Justice Bill introduced in the House of Lords, no assistance was given on what was meant by 'made public'. However, by the Committee Stage of the Bill in the House of Commons, the Government, bowing to pressure, introduced an amendment to correct this. In consequence, the CJA 1993 now gives four circumstances (although these are said not to be exhaustive) in which information is regarded as 'made public'.[17] These circumstances include:

(a) if the information is published in accordance with the rules of a regulated market for the purpose of informing investors and their professional advisers;
(b) if the information is contained in records which, by virtue of any enactment, are given to inspection by the public;
(c) if the information can be readily acquired by those likely to deal in any securities to which the information relates or of an issuer to which the information relates; or
(d) if the information is derived from information which has been made public.

In addition, the CJA 1993 provides five circumstances when information may be treated as having been made public, even though it has not.[18] These are where:

(a) it can be acquired only by persons exercising diligence or expertise;
(b) it is communicated to a section of the public and not to the public at large;
(c) it can be acquired only by observation;
(d) it is communicated only on payment of a fee; or
(e) it is published only outside the UK.

Information published in accordance with the rules of a regulated market
The fact that mere publication of information causes it to cease to have the character of inside information is a little curious since the simple fact of publication will not deprive the insider of his advantage because the market will take time to absorb the information. Until the market has absorbed the information the price is unlikely to reflect the information fully. This is not something which is likely to occur immediately on publication. Accordingly, transactions by insiders before the market has assimilated the information has led to liability in the US[19] and it was probably not safe for insiders to deal immediately on announcement under the Company Securities (Insider Dealing) Act 1985.[20] The price had to adjust to the information first before dealing could take place. Had the definition not been provided in the CJA 1993, it is probable that insiders could not safely deal until the information were made public and had a significant effect on the price. In other words, they would have to wait for the market to assimilate the information. This is probably how the EC Directive on Insider Dealing is to be interpreted.[21]

The definition now provided has the advantage of clarity, since waiting for the market to absorb the news, while theoretically pure, has the disadvantage of providing uncertainty as to the time when insiders may deal.

However, to allow insiders to deal on publication of the information gives insiders an advantage over the rest of the market as they can, so to speak, be ready at the starting blocks the instant the information becomes public and before it has had its full impact on price. In the US, it has been held that insiders may not deal until the market has absorbed the information,[22] on the basis that at the stage of publication the public has not had time to make an informed investment judgment.

Under the CJA 1993 the procedure for notifying information to The Stock Exchange[23] would appear to have the following effect. The information which issuers wish to notify must be delivered in the form of an announcement to the Company Announcements Office. The Stock Exchange then arranges for the prompt publication of announcements through its Regulatory News Service. It is at this point, when, for example, there is an announcement on TOPIC, that it would appear that the information will be 'made public' for the purposes of the CJA 1993.

The Regulatory News Service operates between 7.30 am and 6.00 pm and announcements notified up until 5.30 pm are released on the day of receipt. The Stock Exchange rules provide that no information must be given to a third party before it is given to the Company Announcements Office. However, if announcements are made outside the operational hours of the Regulatory News Service the information must be given to two or more UK national newspapers and to two news services to ensure adequate coverage. It must also be lodged with the Company Announcements Office no later than it is given to the other parties. In these circumstances, the information would appear to have been made public on publication of the newspapers.

Information contained in records open to inspection by the public
Information will be regarded as being made public if it is contained on records which, by virtue of any enactment, are open to inspection by the public. This covers registers set up under statute, such as companies' or patents' registers or in publications such as in the *Official Gazette*.[24]

Information readily acquired by people 'likely to deal' in securities
Information is made public where it can be readily acquired by those likely to deal in any securities to which or to whose issuer the information relates.[25]

The phrase 'likely to deal' in securities appears to have its origin in the Company Securities (Insider Dealing) Act 1985 definition of 'unpublished price-sensitive information'.[26] Although it could be argued that the phrase only embraces the market professionals who deal in the securities, such as market markers who are clearly 'likely to deal', it is also possible that it refers to the market in the shares.[27] If information can be readily acquired by the market, that information is already likely to have made its price impact and is, therefore, not properly to be regarded as inside information. Thus, it is treated as having been 'made public'.

Information derived from information made public
Information is made public if it is derived from information which has been made public.[28] In some ways this is obvious, although, clearly, expert analysis of information, having regard to many other factors, may itself unearth matters which are not in the public domain.

A US court has conveniently summarised the problem, which the CJA 1993 now addresses:[29]

'A skilled analyst with knowledge of the company and the industry may piece seemingly inconsequential data together with public information into a mosaic which reveals material non-public information. Whenever managers and analysts meet elsewhere than in public, there is a risk that the analysts will emerge with knowledge of material information which is not publicly available.'

The danger recounted by that court should not arise in the UK provided that the mosaic which contains the inside information is derived from information which has been made public.

The provisions of the CJA 1993 set out circumstances when information is made public, although they are not exhaustive as to the meaning of that expression.[30] In contrast, further provisions of the CJA 1993 provide for circumstances where information may be treated as having been made public, even though at first sight those circumstances may indicate otherwise. A better way of putting it may be that the fact that the information arises in these circumstances does not necessarily mean that it will not be treated as having been made public. The issue is then a matter for the courts to decide.

The provisions are not entirely satisfactory but the Government claimed in debate[31] that it was important to insert these examples of information which may be treated as having been made public, because many people felt that unless such examples were included information might be considered not to have been made public. Originally, as a result of pressure, the Government wished to issue non-statutory guidance notes. This was abandoned and has been replaced by a statutory basis for what could turn out to be a plea in mitigation.

The Minister used an example of a person doing research in a library who discovers information in an obscure journal which is price sensitive.[32] A court may treat that information as having been made public even though it was never communicated, in the normal sense, to the world at large or, similarly, if the information were communicated only to a section of the public. If a recipient of the information had considered that the information had been made public, the information should be treated as if it had been made public.

In relation to information which can be described as being acquired 'only by observation', the Minister said:

'the point to consider is whether a factory chimney smoking at night could be regarded as public information since everybody could go and see the smoking chimney and take the view that the factory was working overtime or whether it would be regarded as information that had not been promulgated or made public'.[33]

As regards information published only outside the country, the Economic Secretary said that, if information were only published in the *Tonga Evening News*, it would be extremely unlikely to be considered to have been made public, unless the information related to, for example, a local company such as a Tonganese mining company. He considered that information published outside the UK in, for example *Handelsblatt*, might be regarded as made public.[34]

Price sensitivity

The final aspect of the definition of 'inside information' is the price sensitivity of the information. The test is that if the information was made public it would be likely to have a significant effect on the securities. This is the most essential feature of the statutory definition of inside information, since it is this criterion, rather than the issue of how qualitative the information actually is, which really matters and which, at the end of the day, will be the determining factor when a jury considers whether information is inside information.

The test of price sensitivity introduces an hypothesis, because this issue can only strictly be tested at the moment of the deal when, by definition, the information is not known to the public and can have no price impact. In many cases where the insider has dealt close to the time when the information has been made public, evidence of the price sensitivity can be shown by the effect of the information on the market.[35] However, in some cases, because of general market conditions, the behaviour of the price on disclosure of the information may not be a reliable guide to price sensitivity. Accordingly, in one US case,[36] it was held that the fact that a company's shares dropped 11¾ points on disclosure of information did not establish price sensitivity in view of the fact that a substantial decline in the company's shares was not uncommon in its recent history and that several other reasons accounted for a decline in the company's share price. There will, of course, be cases where the matter should be dealt with by expert evidence.[37]

What must be judged is whether the effect likely to be made on the price of the securities is significant and, for this purpose, 'price' includes value.[38] What is or is not significant will vary depending on the circumstances and, while it is clear that a significant price change will only come about after events of an 'extraordinary' nature, such an approach merely puts into different words the same concept without analysis. It is, in fact, impossible to analyse this concept by reference to quantification.

In the absence of any further guidance from the CJA 1993 a court must propound a 'reasonable investor' test relative to the securities in question and leave the matter to the jury. In one US case,[39] it was held that in order for information to be price sensitive there must be substantial likelihood that the disclosure of the fact would have been viewed by the investor as having significantly altered the total mix of information made available. In a Singapore case,[40] it was held that information will become price sensitive if it is information which would influence the ordinary reasonable investor to buy or sell the security in question.

This approach has commended itself to the Australian legislature and has been included in recent legislation on insider dealing[41] as follows:

> '. . . a reasonable person would be taken to expect information to have a material effect on the price or value of securities of a body corporate if the information

would, or would be likely to, influence persons who commonly invest in securities in deciding whether or not to subscribe for, buy or sell the first mentioned securities'.

However, such approaches do not really help. It would appear that, except in the most blatantly obvious case, there must be careful analysis of the evidence supporting what is alleged to be a significant effect on any price.

NOTES

1   *SEC v Texas Gulf Sulphur* 401 F 2d 833 (2d Cir 1968) at p 848.
2   Parliamentary Debates, House of Commons, Standing Committee A, debate on the Companies Bill, 6 December 1979, col 394.
3   CJA 1993, s 56(1).
4   Company Securities (Insider Dealing) Act 1985, s 10.
5   Council Directive (89/592/EEC), Art 1(1).
6   Parliamentary Debates, House of Lords, 3 December 1992, col 1495.
7   The word 'prospects' is also used in s 146(1) of the FSA 1986, dealing with the general duty of disclosure in listing particulars. This was why it was used in the insider dealing legislation. Parliamentary Debates, House of Lords, 3 December 1992, col 1495.
8   See CJA 1993, s 57(2)(a)(ii) and p 40.
9   The example is given of news of the electoral success of a political party hostile to business, in an article by Klaus J Hopt 'The European Insider Dealing Directive' (1990) 27 CMLR 51. The view in the text may not be the view of the Government. The Earl of Caithness (Minister of State), in discussing what is now CJA 1993, s 63(1), appeared to indicate that security matters concerning the Government's policy with respect to interest rates were within the scope of the CJA 1993 (Parliamentary Debates, House of Lords, 19 November 1992, col 776). However, insofar as these matters affect securities or issuers of securities generally, they cannot be inside information.
10 Parliamentary Debates, House of Lords, 3 December 1992, col 1501 (per the Earl of Caithness).
11 *Ryan v Triguboff* [1976] 1 NSWLR 588 at p 596, per Lee J.
12 Ibid at 597. Compare *Commissioner for Corporate Affairs v Green* [1978] VR 505 at p 511, per McInerney J, where the absence of the word 'specific' in legislation was said to allow an inference to be drawn about information.
13 *Public Prosecutor v Choudhury* [1980] 1 MLJ 76 at p 78 (Singapore).
14 As in *Green v Charterhouse Group of Canada Ltd* 12 OR 2d 280 (1976) where the Court of Appeal in Ontario held such information to be specific even though it may not have been worthy of credence or not have been of sufficient weight to justify any positive action by the board (at p 306, per Arrup JA).
15 Parliamentary Debates, House of Commons, Standing Committee B, 10 June 1993, col 174.
16 Ibid, col 175.
17 CJA 1993, s 58(2).
18 Ibid, s 59(3).
19 *SEC v Texas Gulf Sulphur Co* 401 F 2d 833 (2d Cir 1968); *SEC v MacDonald* 699 F 2d 47 (1st Cir 1982).

20   Under s 10 of the Company Securities (Insider Dealing) Act 1985 the information has to be generally known to those persons who are accustomed or would be likely to deal in those securities. There are various views on this provision. It has been said that it requires the information to be generally known to market professionals (see P Arrisman *Insider Trading Legislation for Australia* (National Companies and Securities Commission, Canberra, 1986) at fn 674); that dissemination of information throughout the investing public is not required (see B Rider *Insider Trading* (Jordans, 1983) at p 23); that the market must have internalised the information (see M Ashe and L Counsell *Insider Trading* (Fourmat, 1990) at p 88); and that the information must be fully reflected in the price of the securities (J Suter *The Regulation of Insider Dealing in Britain* (Butterworths, 1989) at p 100).

21   See Klaus J Hopt 'The European Insider Dealing Directive' (1990) 27 CMLR 51. The recital to the Directive speaks of investors being 'placed on an equal footing'.

22   *SEC v Texas Gulf Sulphur Co* 401 F 2d 833 (2d Cir 1968).

23   *The Listing Rules*, Ch 9.

24   Parliamentary Debates, House of Commons, Standing Committee B, 10 June 1993, col 184 (per the Economic Secretary).

25   CJA 1993, s 58(2)(c).

26   Company Securities (Insider Dealing) Act 1985, s 10(b).

27   See n 20 above.

28   CJA 1993, s 58(2)(d).

29   *Elkind v Liggett & Myers Inc* 635 F 2d 156 (2d Cir 1980) at p 165.

30   CJA 1993, s 58(1).

31   Parliamentary Debate, House of Commons, Standing Committee B, 10 June 1993, col 184 (per the Economic Secretary).

32   Ibid, col 183.

33   Ibid, col 184.

34   Ibid, col 183.

35   See *Elkind v Liggett & Myers Inc* 635 F 2d 156 (2d Cir 1980) and the comments of Knox J in *Chase Manhattan Equities Ltd v Goodman* [1991] BCLC 897 at p 931.

36   *SEC v Bausch & Lomb* 565 F 2d 8 (2d Cir 1977).

37   *Public Prosecutor v Alan Ng Poh Meng* [1990] 1 MLJ v (Singapore) was one such case.

38   CJA 1993, s 56(3).

39   *TSC Industries v Northway* 426 US 438 (1976).

40   *Public Prosecutor v Allan Ng Poh Meng* (above).

41   Corporation Act 1989, s 1002C, inserted by Sch 4 to the Corporation Legislation Amendment Act 1991.

WHO IS AN INSIDER?

The principal category of insider under the Company Securities (Insider Dealing) Act 1985 was defined by reference to a 'connection' with a company.[1] That connection was forged in one of two ways.[2] First, if the individual was a director of the company concerned or a related company and secondly, if the individual was an officer (other than a director) or employee of the company or a related company, or occupied a position involving a professional relationship between himself (or his employer or a company of which he was a director) and the first company or a related company, which, in either case, might reasonably have been expected to have given him access to inside information in relation to either company.

Under the provisions of the CJA 1993 there is no requirement that an insider has such a connection, although, clearly, true insiders, such as corporate officers, will have that connection as a matter of fact. Instead, a person will have information as an insider only if:

(a) the information is, and he knows that it is, inside information; and
(b) he has the information and he knows that he has it, from an inside source.[3]

The CJA 1993 goes on to provide that a person has information from an inside source only if:

(a) he has the information through being a director, employee or shareholder of an issuer of securities or has access to the information by virtue of his employment office or profession; or
(b) the direct or indirect source of his information is a person within paragraph (a).[4]

Three distinct classes of persons are embraced, namely the so-called true insiders (directors, employees and shareholders of the body which issued the securities), those on the periphery of that body (such as professionals who gain access to the information) and, finally, tippees of the information.

Compared with the Company Securities (Insider Dealing) Act 1985 there are three major extensions of the concept of who is an insider under the CJA 1993. First, the net goes wider than companies and now embraces public sector bodies.[5] Secondly, shareholders are included for the first time. Thirdly, a simple access to information test replaces the need under the previous legislation to be connected with a company. These additions are caused by the provisions of the EC Directive on Insider Dealing.[6]

Public sector bodies

A local government officer of a district council will, for the first time, be within the ambit of the legislation, in relation to the council's securities. An employee of a foreign government will also be covered, in relation to that government's securities, as will a UK minister or civil servant in relation to gilts.

Shareholders

It is, perhaps, curious that all shareholders should appear to be regarded as insiders. In the US, for example (which is, admittedly, based on case-law rather than on statute), only controlling shareholders are regarded as insiders. This is because such persons are likely, given their power, to have a similar degree of access to information as a director.[7] A shareholder not having such control is unlikely to be in that position and consequently is effectively excluded from UK legislation although remaining, normally, within it.

Access to information

On the periphery of the issuer, are people who may, following US precedent, be termed 'temporary insiders'. These people, whilst being outsiders, may gain access to information by virtue of their position. Typically, those included will be lawyers, accountants, merchant bankers and other professionals with whom companies and other issuers deal.[8] However, the class need not be restricted to them. Office cleaners, temporary secretaries, postmen, company printers and many others could potentially be regarded as having access to information by virtue of their employment. Against this, the provision is only aimed at those whose function it is to have the information. If, in the course of cleaning the issuer's windows, a window cleaner obtains inside information, he can hardly be said to have gained access to it by virtue of his employment. The information will have been gained through a frolic of his own and have come to him incidentally in the course of his employment.[9]

The fact that the CJA 1993 no longer requires an insider to be determined by a 'connection' to an issuer, as was the situation under the Company Securities (Insider Dealing) Act 1985, could be argued to have extended insider dealing liability considerably. This view is supported by the fact that the CJA 1993 imposes liability by reference to informational advantage rather than by reference to status.

The most extreme case of liability by reference to informational advantage arose a few years ago in a US case concerning the 'Heard on the Street' column in the *Wall Street Journal*.[10] In that case, R Foster Winans, a columnist, gave other individuals advance information about the contents of his column in the newspaper. It was known that favourable mention of any share in that column would influence the price beneficially. Profits were therefore made by dealing in advance of the publication of the column on the basis of information to be contained in it. Significantly, the information in the columns was not received from any insider of a corporation. It was simply the view of the journalist who wrote it. For reasons of US law, Winans was convicted of insider dealing, largely, it would seem, on the basis that he had taken confidential business information from the *Wall Street Journal*.

It has been suggested[11] that under UK law, which has now based insider liability on informational advantage rather than by connection to an issuer, Mr Winans would also be liable in the UK. Such a view, however, would not appear to be correct for the following reasons.

The statutory definition requires, as we have seen, inside information to come from an inside source. An individual will have inside information from an inside source if, for example, he has it through being a director or he has access to it by virtue, for example, of his employment.

It is unlikely that a court would hold that information generated by an employee himself would be obtained through having 'access' to it.[12] For there to be access to information a court would probably hold that the information must have an existence independent of the person who is accessing it. Thus, a columnist expressing influential views on stocks is unlikely to be regarded as holding that information as an insider.

On the other hand, a court would be unlikely to hold that the information to which access may be gained is only the information which another individual may have by being the director, employee or shareholder of the issuer. It goes wider than what may be termed 'issuer-generated' information.

It may be, therefore, that while the influential columnist does not have the information which he generates as an insider, the sub-editor or the printer who sees it is in a different situation. They will have had access to it by virtue of their employment and would therefore seem to have that information as an insider. If that information is specific or precise then, if it is not public and is price sensitive in relation to a security, it will be inside information.

The practical consequences of this can be illustrated by looking at an example used elsewhere in this book.[13] To repeat the facts briefly, Airline A plans to give up two of its routes on which the only competition is Airline B. To have information about Airline A could arise in an employment situation where the employer, to use the Company Securities (Insider Dealing) Act 1985 terminology, has a connection with Airline A. However, under that Act, unlike the CJA 1993, that employee would never have been constrained from buying Airline B's shares unless the information related to a transaction between Airline A and Airline B. The effect of the CJA 1993 is to make him an 'insider' of Airline B by virtue of the information he holds.

The broadening of the base of the legislation has given rise to concern about the position of analysts.[14] It is common for analysts to have close contact with a company as part of their functions of analysing published information. There is likely to be widespread agreement that analysts' contacts with company management should not become, in the words of one US court, 'a fencing match conducted on a tightrope'.[15]

The Government has said[16] that it attaches considerable importance to good communications between companies and the City and that the practice of explaining the details of company operations to analysts and fund managers has an important part to play in this. However, with that positive statement has come the warning that price-sensitive information ought not to be selectively disclosed and that disclosure of price-sensitive information in confidence poses problems for all concerned. An analyst could have been in breach of the Company Securities (Insider Dealing) Act 1985[17] if he were to use such information prior to publication. Indeed, the view of the Government is that if company representatives, on reviewing what has been said at a meeting, believe that they may have unwittingly revealed some unpublished, price-sensitive information, they should immediately disclose that information to The Stock Exchange for publication to the whole market.

It should be noted that a person will only have information as an insider if he has knowledge in two respects – first, if he knows that it is inside information and secondly, if he knows that he has it from the relevant inside source. It is unlikely that the burden of proof in showing this will prove difficult when dealing with directors, professionals or most employees. However, it is possible that a junior employee may not know that the information is inside information (at least it should not, if one is considering a prosecution, be taken as a foregone conclusion that he does know of its quality).

NOTES

1   Company Securities (Insider Dealing) Act 1985, s 1.
2   Ibid, s 9.
‑3   CJA 1993, s 57(1).
4   Ibid, s 57(2).
5   'Issuer of securities' includes any body, whether incorporated or not and wherever it is incorporated or constituted, and public sector bodies, which means any Government, local authority, central bank of a sovereign state wherever they are and any international

organisation of which the UK or any other member of the European Community is a member (CJA 1993, s 60(2) and (3)).

6   Council Directive (89/592/EEC), Art 1(2) and 2.1.

7   For example, *Speed v Transamerica Corp* 71F Supp 457 (D Del 1947).

8   This is unlikely, necessarily, to require a commercial basis; for an interesting factual example see *SEC v Ingram* 694 F Supp 1437 (C D Cal 1988), although the basis of liability is different. The classic US access case concerned a security printer (*US v Chiarella* 445 US 222 (1980)).

9   It will be recalled that in the film *Wall Street* the 'hero' Bud Fox, played by Charlie Sheen, became part owner in an office cleaning company in order to 'steal' inside information for a law firm. In English law, such information would not be regarded as stolen as something physical has to be taken in order to charge theft (*Oxford v Moss* (1978) 68 Cr App R 183). However, the tippee provision may be relevant to such a person, see p 45.

10 *US v Winans* 612 F Supp 827 (SDNY 1985); *US v Carpenter* 791 F 2d 1024 (2d Cir 1986); *Carpenter v US* 484 US 19 (1987). For Mr Winans' own account, see R Foster Winans *Trading Secrets* (Macmillan, London 1987). See also *Zweig v Hearst* 594 F 2d 1261 (9th Cir 1979).

11 For example, the paper presented by Mr N Walmsley to the Bar Association for Commerce Finance and Industry and the Wilde Sapte Seminar on Insider Dealing, 29 April 1993; a view which finds support in the DTI Consultative Document 'The Law on Insider Dealing' (December 1989).

12 Compare rule 28(3)(a) of the SIB Core Conduct of Business Rules and the commentary by M Blair *Financial Services, The New Core Rules* (Blackstone, 1991) at p 124. However, see para 2.26 of the DTI Consultative Document *The Law on Insider Dealing* (December 1989) for a statement which assumes the contrary view.

13 See p 30.

14 For example, this view has been expressed in relation to CJA 1993, s 60(4) (Parliamentary Debates, House of Commons, Standing Committee B, 10 June 1993, col 196 (per Peter Ainsworth MP)).

15 To quote *SEC v Bausch & Lomb Inc* 565 F 2d 8 (2d Cir 1977) at p 9.

16 See para 2.5 of the DTI Consultative Document *The Law on Insider Dealing* (December 1989); reiterated by the Economic Secretary in Parliamentary Debates, House of Commons, Standing Committee B, 10 June 1993, col 198.

17 In *Lord Advocate v Mackie* (1993) *Financial Times*, March 31, an analyst to whom information was passed was convicted of the counselling or procuring offence contrary to s 1(7) of the Companies Securities (Insider Dealing) Act 1985. Mr Mackie was given information about the forthcoming issue of a profits warning by a company from its chairman and was indicted for counselling or procuring two of his colleagues to deal in those shares. At the time of writing, an appeal against conviction is pending.

TIPPEES

Tippee liability[1] is the third category of insider liability[2] created by the CJA 1993. A person has information as an insider if the direct or indirect source of his information is a person who falls within one of the other two categories of insider, namely, directors, employees or shareholders of issuers or those who have access to inside information by virtue of their employment, office or profession. As with other insiders, to be liable for insider dealing a tippee must know that the information is inside information and he must know that he has it from an inside source.

Not all tippees and few sub-tippees will know that information is inside information. In fact the classic 'tip' will not contain inside information at all, but will be, for example, 'buy X Ltd' or 'sell Y Ltd'. In such circumstances, no inside information will have been imparted so that while the individual who gave the tip will have committed an offence[3] the tippee would appear to be outside the provision as he will not have 'information as an insider' even though he knows the tip comes from an inside source.

Where sub-tippees are involved in circumstances where information has passed through several hands and has, as a result, become diluted, exaggerated or changed, it may be difficult to establish that the tippee has inside information. Quite apart from proving the state of knowledge, it may also be difficult in some cases to prove that the information, by this stage possibly very inaccurate, is, in fact, inside information at all. Moreover, even when the information which has passed through several hands is accurate it may not be easy to show that the sub-tippee knows that he has the inside information from an inside source.

The difficulties can be seen by looking at the facts of the US case *US v Musella*.[4] An employee of a large Wall Street law firm regularly passed inside information, through a broker, to Dominick Musella, who then tipped his brother John Musella, a New York City policeman, who in turn recommended share purchases to two of his colleagues on the police force, O'Neill and Martin. Neither O'Neill nor Martin knew either the identity or the position of the original source of the information. Moreover, they did not know the specific basis for the tip. Not even Dominick Musella knew the identity or the position of the source of the information as that person was referred to, in conversations with a broker who acted as go-between, as 'the Goose that laid the Golden Egg'.

Both the Musellas and O'Neill and Martin were held criminally liable for insider dealing and the message from the court in the US appears to be that a person receiving suspicious information cannot avoid enquiry and then expect to raise a defence of lack of knowledge.

Looking at these brief facts and applying the CJA 1993, it is suggested that the following would result.

Dominick Musella appears to have had the information, knew that the information was inside information and also knew that there was an indirect source of his information, but did not know either the source's identity or his position. It is unlikely that a court would hold that knowledge of identity was crucial.[5] However, how is it known that 'the Goose' is an inside source being either a director, employee or shareholder of the issuer or a person having access to the information by virtue of his employment, office or profession? For example 'the Goose' may, himself, have been a tippee so that Dominick did not know of any other source.

It is unlikely that it would have to be shown that 'the Goose' was an inside source and that Dominick knew this. Whatever 'the Goose's' position or whatever the true insider's identity the circumstances of receiving the inside information regularly from 'the Goose', via the broker, would be enough, unless rebutted, to show the requisite degree of knowledge.

The position of John Musella may be equivocal but it is clear that neither O'Neill nor Martin knew what the information was. Given that it must be proved that they knew the information was inside information and that a recommendation to buy shares cannot, in these circumstances, be inside information it is submitted that O'Neill and Martin would be acquitted in the UK under the CJA 1993.

It is sometimes mistakenly thought that the establishment of tippee liability is dependent on the liability of the individual who tips. This is clearly not the case. It may be that in the course of negotiations inside information may be passed bona fide to another person.[6] However, if the recipient of the information then deals he will, in all likelihood, commit an offence. Thus, an individual who overhears inside information will have that information as an insider if he knows it is inside information and knows that he has it from an inside source.[7] Similarly, an individual who takes inside information, knowing it is from an inside source, will attract tippee liability.

Given that (unlike the Company Securities (Insider Dealing) Act 1985) the inside source need have no connection with the issuer whose securities are concerned, tippee liability has been extended under the CJA 1993. Thus, in a situation where the person disclosing the information has access to it through their employment it will no longer be necessary to show, as it was previously, that the person was in a position which might reasonably be expected to give him access.[8] Under the Company Securities (Insider Dealing) Act 1985 this was necessary to establish that person as a connected person and, among other things, to establish the tippee's liability.[9] The basis of liability has been simplified and the scope of the tippee offence extended.

NOTES

1 The Criminal Justice Bill, when first presented to the House of Lords, actually used the word 'tippee'. The word drew strong opposition from their Lordships (see Parliamentary Debates, House of Lords, 19 November 1992, cols 756–767). The word was removed before the Bill left the House of Lords (ibid, 3 December 1992, col 1496).

2 CJA 1993, s 57(2)(b).

3 Under CJA 1993, s 52(2)(a). See p 51.

4 678 F Supp 1060 (SDNY 1988); see also *SEC v Musella* 748 F Supp 1028 (SDNY 1989).

5 But see *Attorney-General's Reference (No 1 of 1988)* [1989] AC 971 at 993B, where Lord Lowry seems to indicate, in relation to the phrase 'knowingly obtained' in s 1(3) of the Company Securities (Insider Dealing) Act 1985, that the tippee must know for whom he obtained the inside information.

6 As, for example, in *Public Prosecutor v Allen Ng Poh Meng* (1990) MLJ v (Singapore) and in *R v Fisher* (1988) 4 BCC 360 (on appeal, sub nom *Attorney General's Reference (No 1 of 1988)* [1989] AC 971). Such a disclosure may be in the proper performance of duties and not come within CJA 1993, s 52(2)(b).

7 A classic example is to be found in *SEC v Switzer* 590 F Supp 756 (WED Okla 1984), although for reasons of US law there was no liability.

8 Company Securities (Insider Dealing) Act 1985, s 10(b).

9 This was part of the reason for the direction to acquit in *R v Kean and Floyd* (1991) (unreported).

THE DEALING OFFENCE

The two essential requirements for the dealing offence are that:

(a) an individual must have information as an insider; and
(b) the insider must deal in securities that are price-affected securities in
     relation to the information.[1]

In relation to inside information, price-affected securities are securities
the prices of which will be likely to be significantly affected if information
relating to them is made public.[2]

Accordingly, if an insider has inside information he must not deal in the
securities to which that information relates. The CJA 1993 defines 'dealing
in securities' quite broadly. Any acquisition or disposal of a security is
covered,[3] including an agreement to acquire[4] or dispose of[5] a security and
the entering into a contract[6] which creates the security or the bringing to
an end of such a contract.[7] Moreover, such acquisitions or disposals are
within the definition whether they are made by an individual as principal
or as agent.

The relevant time at which to consider whether or not an offence has
been committed would appear to be at the time of agreement to acquire or
dispose of the security. If, at that time, the individual had inside information about these securities he will have committed an offence. However, if
he received inside information only after making the agreement he will
probably not have contravened the provision if he completes the deal and
actually acquires or disposes of the securities.[8] On the other hand, if the
individual had the inside information at the time when he agreed to
acquire or dispose of the security it would seem that he will still have
committed an offence, even if he does not complete the bargain.[9]

The acquisition or disposal may be made by an individual acting either as
principal or agent. Accordingly, if an agent has inside information, he will
be within the scope of the offence if he deals in the relevant securities even
though, in the direct sense, he will not gain from the transaction.[10] The
logic of this is plain in circumstances where the agent is engaging in the
transaction to benefit his principal. This is simple insider dealing and the
fact that the individual deals as agent and not principal is irrelevant.
However, where the agent deals on an execution basis only, such an
approach hardly seems justified and is unfair to the principal who gave the
instruction if the agent then feels inhibited from processing the order.
Fortunately, it appears that a defence deals with this situation so that the
agent may act on instructions notwithstanding that, incidentally, he has
inside information.[11]

A person is also regarded as dealing in securities if he procures, directly or indirectly, an acquisition or disposal of the securities by another person.[12] Such procurement by a person may occur if the security is acquired or disposed of by a person who is his agent, his nominee or a person acting at his direction in relation to the acquisition or disposal,[13] although these examples are not exhaustive.[14] This aspect of the definition of 'dealing in securities' is designed to cover situations where a person relies on inside information without purchasing or selling the securities himself – hence the reference to transactions through an agent or a nominee.

Transactions at another person's direction are targeted at a person who, as a sole shareholder, uses his influence over a company to deal in shares.[15] Disquiet was expressed in the House of Commons Standing Committee during the passage of the Criminal Justice Bill at the scope of the phrase 'a person who is acting at his direction'.[16] It was suggested that the phrase could include, by mistake, a person who has inside information but whose investment portfolio is handled by someone else on a discretionary basis. For example, a fund manager may deal at his own discretion in the securities to which his principal's inside information relates, rendering the principal guilty of an offence, notwithstanding the principal's lack of knowledge of the deal.

The Economic Secretary, in reply, stated that whilst it was possible that a person who has handed over the management of his investment portfolio to another may be considered to have procured particular dealings, 'it may well be that'[17] a person who gives a general direction to another to manage all his affairs would not be considered to have directed and, therefore, to have procured dealings in securities which the person with the general management of the affairs had decided upon. The Minister also stated that, in cases where a court might consider that in such circumstances a person had procured an acquisition, the holder of the shares would, if he had genuinely not influenced the dealing, have a statutory defence.[18]

NOTES

1   CJA 1993, s 52(1).
2   Ibid, s 56(2).
3   Ibid, s 55(1)(a).
4   Ibid, s 55(2)(a).
5   Ibid, s 55(3)(a).
6   Ibid, s 55(2)(b).
7   Ibid, s 55(3)(b).
8   An alternative way to approach this issue is to rely on the defence in CJA 1993, s 53(1)(c). See p 54.
9   None of the defences in CJA 1993, s 53(1) would appear to cover this situation. See p 54.
10 Except for his commission, if any.

11   CJA 1993, s 53(1)(c). See p 54. Compare s 3(2) of the Company Securities (Insider Dealing) Act 1985 dealing with facilitating the completion or carrying out of transactions.
12   CJA 1993, s 55(1)(b).
13   Ibid, s 55(4).
14   Ibid, s 55(5).
15   Parliamentary Debates, House of Commons, Standing Committee B, 10 June 1993, col 171 (per the Economic Secretary).
16   Ibid, col 167 (per Peter Ainsworth MP).
17   Ibid, cols 171 and 172.
18   Under CJA 1993, s 53(1)(c). See p 54.

THE ENCOURAGEMENT OFFENCE

The gravamen of the encouragement offence is to encourage another person to deal, knowing or having reasonable cause to believe that the person receiving the encouragement would deal in securities in the circumstances covered by the dealing offence.[1]

It is not necessary, in order for the offence to be committed, for the individual who has information as an insider to tell the other person any of the information. Neither is it necessary that the other person should know that the securities he is encouraged to buy are price-affected securities. The offence will, therefore, embrace the classic tip given by an insider to another, for example 'I strongly recommend you purchase as many X Ords as you can afford', although it is not confined to those situations.

If the insider knows or has reasonable cause to believe that the other person will deal on a regulated market or through or as a professional intermediary the offence will be committed even if, in fact, the other person does not deal. However, in practice, in most cases a deal will be necessary to ensure a conviction.

NOTES

1   CJA 1993, s 52(2)(a).

THE DISCLOSURE OFFENCE

The disclosure offence is committed by an individual, who has information as an insider, if he discloses the information otherwise than in the proper performance of the functions of his employment, office or profession, to another person.[1]

The framing of the offence makes it clear that there will be occasions when it is entirely proper in the performance of an employment, office or profession to disclose inside information. An example of this would be in relation to a purchase of a large tranche of shares. It would be usual practice, and entirely proper in such circumstances, for a merchant banker acting for the vendor to disclose to a bona fide prospective purchaser, during negotiations, information including inside information.[2] The merchant banker would not, in such circumstances, be guilty of an offence even if the recipient of the information breached his confidence and then dealt in the shares.

However, it would not generally be proper for an individual to disclose inside information, which he had in the course of his employment, merely because he did not intend that the recipient of that information should deal on the basis of it. Accordingly, if an analyst had inside information in that capacity it may not be in the proper performance of his duties if he disclosed that information to his employer's investment department or market makers.[3]

The problem for company executives dealing with analysts may become, in the light of the CJA 1993 and in the words of one US court, 'a fencing match conducted on a tightrope'.[4] However, if the company executive did not expect any person to deal as a result of his disclosure to the analyst, he will have a defence.[5]

The position of an individual who discloses inside information of fraud in a company, to enable the recipients of the inside information to sell their securities, may not be so fortunate.[6] His disclosure may safely be made only to the police.

NOTES

1   CJA 1993, s 52(2)(b).

2   Examples can be found in *R v Fisher* (1988) 4 BCC 360 (on appeal, sub nom *Attorney General's Reference (No 1 of 1988)* [1989] AC 971); and *Public Prosecutor v Allen Ng Poh Meng* [1990] MLJ v (Singapore).

3 See *SEC v First Boston Corporation Corp* [1986–87 Transfer Binder] Fed Sec L Rep (CCH) 92, 712 (SDNY 5 May 1986); *R v Kean and Floyd* (1991) (unreported); and see *Lord Advocate v Mackie* (1993) *Financial Times*, March 31.

4 *SEC v Bausch & Lomb Inc* 565 F 2d 8 (2d Cir 1977) at p 9.

5 CJA 1993, s 53(3)(a). See p 55.

6 *Dirks v SEC* 445 US 646 (1983). Mr Dirks was an analyst who received inside information about fraud and discussed it with his clients who sold their shares. He also publicised the information and brought it to the attention of the SEC who then, rather ungratefully, took out administrative proceedings against him. The Supreme Court dismissed these proceedings, but the attitude is unlikely to be as benevolent in the UK.

GENERAL DEFENCES

Statutory defences are provided for each of the insider dealing offences and will succeed if they are proved by the defendant on the balance of probabilities.[1] In respect of the dealing offence[2] and the encouragement offence[3] an individual is not guilty if he shows that he did not, at the time, expect the dealing to result in a profit or to avoid a loss[4] which was attributable to the fact that the information in question was price-sensitive information[5] in relation to the securities. Since the offence is committed at the point of agreement to deal and not on completion (if this is different) the wording of this defence does not appear to allow for the situation where completion does not, in fact, take place. Whereas such an approach can be seen to be appropriate in relation to the encouragement offence, it appears to be a little narrow in respect of the dealing offence. The encouragement will factually have occurred, whether or not a deal takes place, so the expectation at that time is clearly important. However, whatever the technicalities, if the bargain is not completed the deal will not have gone through so that the expectations at the contract stage seem unimportant. Presumably, prosecutions will be rare where completion has not taken place.

A defence is also available to both the dealing offence and the encourage-ment offence where the accused shows that he would still have acted as he did even if he had not had the information.[6] An individual may have been either planning to deal or to encourage someone else to deal anyway. If that is the case, and he can show it, then the fact that he had the inside information should not inhibit him. The inside information may have been received after the plans had been formulated or circumstances may have arisen where, for example, a holding of shares had to be sold notwithstand-ing the possession of inside information. It will, of course, be easier to discharge the burden of proof in the first situation than in the second, although in circumstances of economic compulsion to sell (faced with no other readily realisable property) it would seem possible and right that the defence should also be available in the second situation.

What may be more difficult to prove is that having the inside informa-tion, in circumstances where there was no economic pressure to sell, had no influence on the decision to deal. The timing of the deal will be important unless the defendant can justify the timing of the deal without reference to the inside information a defence is less likely to succeed. Moreover, there is the inherent danger that a jury would be sceptical about such a defence. However, the defence would seem to cover the case of, for example, a trustee who, whilst having inside information about securities, dealt in them on behalf of the trust on the basis of independent advice.

An individual will also be innocent of the dealing offence if he shows that at the time when he dealt in securities he believed, on reasonable grounds, that the information had been disclosed widely enough to ensure that none of those taking part in the dealing would be prejudiced by not having the information.[7] An example of when this defence can be raised is when two parties are in contact with each other and they both have information that can or cannot yet be made public. It is particularly aimed at properly conducted corporate finance transactions,[8] so that, for example, it covers underwriting transactions where both parties know the information. The defence is unlikely to go substantially beyond that, although it might conceivably be available to someone who wrongly, but honestly and reasonably, thought that the information had been made public.

A similar defence is available in relation to the encouragement offence. The accused must show that he believed, on reasonable grounds, that the information had been or would be disclosed, by the time of the deal which he was encouraging, widely enough to ensure that none of those taking part in the dealing would be prejudiced by not having the information.[9]

There are two defences in relation to the disclosure offence which cover situations where no dealing was expected[10] or where the deal was not expected to lead to profit or avoid a loss attributable to the fact that the information was price sensitive.[11] It will be recalled that the defences need not go beyond this because the definition of the offence[12] excludes disclosure of information by an individual in the proper performance of his employment, office or profession.

NOTES

1 CJA 1993, s 53. On the general principle that the burden is on the accused to raise a statutory defence, see *R v Cross* [1991] BCLC 15, a case under the Company Securities (Insider Dealing) Act 1985.
2 CJA 1993, s 53(1)(a).
3 Ibid, s 53(2)(a).
4 Ibid, s 53(b).
5 Inside information is price-sensitive information if the information would, if made public, be likely to have a significant effect on the price of the securities (CJA 1993, s 56(2)).
6 Ibid, s 53(1)(c) and (2)(c).
7 Ibid, s 53(1)(b).
8 Parliamentary Debates, House of Commons, Standing Committee B, 10 June 1993, col 1578 (per the Economic Secretary).
9 CJA 1993, s 53(2)(b).
10 Ibid, s 53(3)(a).
11 Ibid, s 53(3)(b).
12 Ibid, s 52(2)(b).

SPECIAL DEFENCES

Three special defences to the dealing and encouragement offences are provided[1] which may be broadly described as 'market defences'. Two of the defences are specific, one for market makers and one for stabilisation. The other defence generally relates to what has been described as 'market information'.

The market maker's defence

A market maker is a person who holds himself out at all normal times, in compliance with the rules of a regulated market or an approved organisation, as willing to acquire or dispose of securities and is recognised as doing so under these rules.[2] The market maker's defence[3] may be raised where a market maker shows that he acted in good faith either in the course of his business as, or his employment in the business of, a market maker.[4] It is not clear whether this defence is available to a market maker who continues to deal in a share after he has heard or been given information by mistake.[5] The difficulty for a market maker in those circumstances, particularly if his employer is the corporate broker for the share, is that if he withdraws from the market the whole City will know something is about to happen and, if he deals, he may indulge in insider dealing.

The equivalent provision under the Company Securities (Insider Dealing) Act 1985 did not prohibit the market maker from dealing while in possession of inside information if the information was obtained by him in the course of his business and was of a description which it was reasonable to expect him to obtain in the ordinary course of that business.[6] The CJA 1993, by omitting these hurdles, may, in some circumstance, give a market maker a defence where he is wrongly exposed to inside information and continues to deal.[7]

The stabilisation defence

The stabilisation defence will apply if an individual has acted in accordance with the price stabilisation rules.[8] These rules are contained in Part 10 of the Financial Services (Conduct of Business) Rules 1990 made by the Securities and Investments Board[9] and are designed to enable a manager of an issue of securities to go into the market to stabilise or maintain the market price of these securities. The defence to insider dealing is provided so that this activity is not inhibited if carried out in accordance with the rules.

The market information defence

A more general market defence to insider dealing is the market information defence. An individual will not be guilty of insider dealing if he shows that the information which he had was market information and it was reasonable for an individual in his position to have acted as he did, despite having the information as an insider at the time.[10] A typical example of market information is said, by the Economic Secretary to HM Treasury, to be when an individual sells a large block of shares and the publication of that information would have an effect on the share price, as would the knowledge that someone intended to sell the block of shares.[11]

'Market information' is defined extensively in the CJA 1993 but, in broad terms, it is information that someone acquiring or disposing of securities may acquire inevitably as a result of these activities. It is information consisting of one or more of the following facts.[12]

1 Information that securities of a particular kind have been or are to be acquired or disposed of or that their acquisition or disposal is under consideration or the subject of negotiation.

2 Information that securities of a particular kind have not been or are not to be acquired or disposed of.

3 Information concerning the number of securities acquired or disposed of or to be acquired or disposed of or that the acquisition or disposal of such securities is under consideration or the subject of negotiation.

4 Information concerning the price (or range of prices) at which securities have been or are to be acquired or disposed of or the price (or range of prices) at which securities the acquisition or disposal of which is under consideration or the subject of negotiation.

5 Information concerning the identity of the persons involved or likely to be involved in any capacity in an acquisition or disposal.

The CJA 1993 provides[13] that, in determining whether it is reasonable for an individual to do any act, despite having market information at the time, the content of the information, the circumstances in which he first had the information, and in what capacity, and the capacity in which he now acts will all be taken into account. In deciding whether it would be reasonable to use market information in specific circumstances, a practitioner should be guided by the rules of the body which authorises him to conduct investment business or the rules of the market in which he is dealing.[14]

A further market information defence is available[15] where an individual shows that he acted in connection with an acquisition or disposal, which was under consideration or the subject of negotiation, with a view to facilitating the accomplishment of the acquisition or disposal and the information arose directly out of his involvement.

NOTES

1 CJA 1993, s 53(4).
2 CJA 1993, Sch 1, para 1(2). An approved organisation means on international securities, self-regulating organisation approved under Sch 1, para 25B to the FSA 1986. Regulated markets are provided for by CJA 1993, s 60(1) and the draft Insider Dealing (Regulated Markets and Securities) Order 1993. See Appendix 2.
3 Ibid, Sch 1, para 1.
4 Ibid, Sch 1, para 1(1). In the first draft of the Criminal Justice Bill there was a defence if the person was employed by a market maker. This was amended to make clear that the defence was only to apply to a market maker's market making employees (Parliamentary Debates, House of Commons, Standing Committee B, 15 June 1993, col 216 (per the Economic Secretary)).
5 The facts of *R v Kean and Floyd* (1991) (unreported). The point did not arise at trial by reference to the former provision in s 3(d) of the Company Securities (Insider Dealing) Act 1985 as there was a direction to acquit at the close of the Crown's case.
6 Ibid, s 3(d).
7 He may also have a defence under CJA 1993, s 53(1)(c).
8 CJA 1993, Sch 1, para 5.
9 Under s 48(7) of the FSA 1986, conformity with the rules prevents a market manipulation offence being committed under s 47(2) of that Act.
10 CJA 1993, Sch 1, para 2(1).
11 Parliamentary Debates, House of Commons, Standing Committee B, 15 June 1993, col 216.
12 CJA 1993, Sch 1, para 4.
13 Ibid, Sch 1, para 2(2).
14 Parliamentary Debates, House of Commons, Standing Committee B, 15 June 1993, col 217 (per the Economic Secretary).
15 CJA 1993, Sch 1, para 3.

TERRITORIAL SCOPE

The CJA 1993 requires a territorial link between the insider offence and the UK; the object of this being to provide a framework for preventing two forms of insider dealing in the UK. These are by insider dealing on markets in the UK or by insider dealing on other regulated markets through the use of professional intermediaries based in the UK.[1]

To commit the dealing offence:[2]

(a) an individual must be in the UK at the time of any act forming part of the dealing;
(b) the regulated market on which the dealing occurs must be one regulated in the UK; or
(c) the professional intermediary must have been within the UK at the time when he is alleged to have done anything by means of which the offence is alleged to have been committed.

It would appear, therefore, that the following examples of deals in price-affected securities are within the scope of the CJA 1993 if the dealer is an insider:

(a) dealing in securities of a UK company on The London Stock Exchange;
(b) dealing in the securities of a French company[3] on The London Stock Exchange;
(c) telephoning from the UK an order to purchase securities on a company listed in Venice;
(d) dealing in Spanish Government stock on The London Stock Exchange;
(e) who is Irish, relying on a London professional intermediary to deal in shares quoted on the Dublin Stock Exchange;
(f) who is an English resident, relying on a professional intermediary based in Northern Ireland to buy shares listed in Frankfurt;
(g) who is a UK resident, agreeing, by telephone, to make a contract for differences[4] in New York;
(h) who is a French resident, dealing in a French security listed on The London Stock Exchange;
(i) who is a UK resident, procuring his Cayman company to deal in securities on divers markets.

During the House of Lords debate on the Second Reading of the Criminal Justice Bill, Lord Williams of Mostyn QC[5] offered the following gratuitous advice to those who wished to avoid UK law on insider dealing.

'Insider, go to Paris upon the bus; sit upon the aeroplane to Maastricht, consider a long weekend in Damascus. I mention Damascus since it is the customary preferred destination for those who risk Pauline conversions – normally described these days as U turns.'

Whilst this statement could be seen as a criticism of the CJA 1993 provisions, it fails to see the practical common sense of the basis of jurisdiction in the CJA 1993. French and Dutch [and Syrian] law has to deal with the examples in the statement above.

The disclosure or encouragement offence will not be committed unless the insider was within the UK when he disclosed the information or encouraged the dealing, or the recipient of the information or encouragement was within the UK when he received the information or encouragement.[6] Accordingly, tipping persons overseas from a UK telephone would, for example, be covered by the insider dealing offence, as would tipping a person within the jurisdiction from a telephone abroad.

NOTES

1 Parliamentary Debates, House of Lords, 19 November 1992, col 774 (per the Earl of Caithness).
2 CJA 1993, s 61(1). Compare, generally, the jurisdiction provisions of Part 1 of the CJA 1993.
3 'Company' includes foreign incorporated company (CJA 1993, s 59(3)(a)).
4 This would, of course, only be a contract for difference falling within CJA 1993, Sch 2, para 7.
5 Parliamentary Debates, House of Lords, 3 November 1992, col 1367.
6 CJA 1993, s 61(2).

PART 3

CIVIL LIABILITY AND ENFORCEMENT

CIVIL LIABILITY

How does civil liability arise?

Unlike many other countries there has always been resistance to the imposition, by statute, of civil liability for insider dealing in the UK.[1] Parliament has taken the view that it is for the courts to fashion appropriate civil remedies and not for the legislature to prescribe them. Whilst judges have shown little sympathy for those who abuse their position by taking advantage of privileged information[2] they can only work within the perimeters of existing rights and obligations. Consequently, there is no indication, except in the area of fiduciary accountability, that an effective civil remedy is in the making. It must be remembered that the purpose of the civil law is primarily to make good a loss. As we have already seen, in the case of most market transactions the marrying of a buyer and seller will, in practice, be random. Thus, even if you can regard the innocent party's disadvantage in dealing with an insider as a loss, whether it would be fair and reasonable for him to be compensated, given the fact that his position is no different from any other in the market who dealt on the same terms, is open to debate. It is this analysis which has led many to conclude that insider dealing is essentially victimless. As we have seen the real victim is the market and, thereby, all those who depend upon it. However, efforts to evolve a civil remedy, according to traditional theories of compensation and restitution for the market and society at large, have proved to be beyond even the ingenuity of US lawyers.

Civil liability presupposes relationships, recognised and identified by law, as appropriately giving rise to a legitimate expectation that the harm in question will not occur without just compensation. Thus, in practical terms, the fashioning of an effective civil remedy for those who happen to deal in the market with insiders, let alone derivative insiders, such as tippers, is most unlikely in the UK. To contemplate such a cause of action would, without statutory intervention, strain traditional concepts of reliance, causation and privacy to the point of fiction. Therefore, in practice civil liability for insider dealing is confined to what are generally described as direct personal transactions, or face-to-face deals, which are executed, in the vast majority of cases, off the markets. It is possible, although exceptional, for a direct transaction to occur on a market, particularly where a substantial block of securities is involved. In practice, there will be such special circumstances surrounding this kind of transaction that the risk of insider abuse should be minimal. Therefore, in examining what prospects there may be for imposing civil liability on a person who has taken advantage of privileged information, we are in practice concerned with off-market deals which involve face-to-face transactions.[3]

Civil liability, in the absence of statutory intervention, may arise in the law of contract, tort or through the application of fiduciary principles. Liability, in a case involving simply the exploitation of inside information as opposed to some element of manipulation, will be based on the failure of the insider to disclose to the party with whom he is dealing the material information in question. The issue will turn upon the circumstances in which an insider, or someone who obtains inside information from a person in a privileged position, will be bound to disclose this information to the party with whom he deals.[4] Indeed, in many instances it is likely that the insider may be under a specific duty to his employer or another to keep the information confidential. This will not necessarily provide the insider with a defence to an allegation that he has breached a duty of disclosure to the person with whom he deals (provided that such a duty has arisen) but it may tend to dissuade a court from finding a duty in the first place, on the basis that the person dealing with him could not reasonably expect full and frank disclosure.[5]

In which circumstances will a person who possesses material information affecting a proposed transaction be bound to disclose it to the person with whom he is dealing? The general rule is caveat emptor – let the buyer beware. With few exceptions, the common law, as the Roman law before it, has never expected a seller to depreciate his own wears; it is for the buyer to exercise caution and, if necessary, to protect himself by inserting into the contract an express stipulation of full disclosure.[6] The scheme of regulation imposed on the financial markets 'gives proper prominence to this time-honoured principle'.[7] There are exceptional circumstances where the courts have accepted that the customs of the market,[8] or the inability of a party to adequately protect himself[9] are such as to justify the imposition of a duty of disclosure. However, there is no indication that the courts would be prepared to find such an exception in the case of dealings on the stock market or in off-market transactions.[10] Thus, as a matter of contract law, mere non-disclosure of price-sensitive information (even if it is obtained in circumstances where the other party could not have access to it) will not constitute misrepresentation and thereby, will not give the other party a remedy in damages or the ability to rescind the transaction.[11] The only protection that the other party will have is to include, during the negotiations leading up to contract, a term requiring the other party to disclose or vouch that he has disclosed all material information. The courts will not generally be prepared to imply such terms or attempt to incorporate such obligations from extraneous sources.

Misrepresentation

If the person possessing the relevant information does more than simply remain reticent, the position may be very different. If he makes a statement, by word or conduct, during the negotiations, which by virtue of an omission to state a material fact renders what he does say misleading, and the other party is misled, the law of misrepresentation becomes relevant.[12] Depending on the circumstance this may give the innocent counterparty a right to damages, rescission and/or an indemnity. By the same token, if the insider makes a statement, which later becomes falsified by a subsequent event, prior to contract, the law imposes a duty upon him to correct what he has said, otherwise his earlier statement becomes a misrepresentation.[13]

Other possible remedies

The law of tort may provide a remedy, in certain circumstances, where a statement has been made which has induced another to act in such a manner as to occasion him loss, and that statement has been made either negligently or fraudulently. The point to note, however, is that mere failure to disclose information will still not be actionable unless there is a duty to disclose the relevant facts.[14] Thus, it does not matter how dishonest an insider might be in wishing harm on the person with whom he deals, if he is under no duty of care to that person, or under no duty to make proper disclosure, he will not be liable.[15] In most situations, there will be no duty to take care and, as we have already emphasised, a person cannot be charged with fraudulent non-disclosure of information if he was under no duty to disclose it in the first place. Therefore, in practice, the matter must be dealt with under the law of contract. It has been contended that insofar as the criminal law and various self-regulatory rules impose a duty on certain persons not to take advantage on inside information, an insider, by dealing, represents that he is not in possession of information which would breach these obligations. By trading, he represents, by his conduct, that he is not in possession of material price-sensitive information which has not been suitably disclosed.[16] Whilst such notions have found limited favour in the US, given the added dimension of appropriately drafted statutory provisions, it is unlikely that a UK court will be so adventuresome at this stage in the development of UK law.[17] However, it remains open to a judge to determine that anti-insider dealing rules are so prevalent in the markets that by dealing, an investor impliedly represents compliance to those rules.

Equity, and to some extent the law of tort, recognises certain special relationships, borne of confidence and proximity, in which it is right and proper for the courts to impose exceptional obligations on those involved. The law of contract will also recognise that in such relationships the ordinary principles of the common law and, in particular, caveat emptor, may not be applicable. Such relationships will rarely be encountered in transactions involving insider abuse. To impose an obligation of fair dealing and disclosure during the negotiations leading up to the transaction in question, the special relationship must be a pre-existing one, and unless there is resort to exotic and unconvincing theories, a special relationship cannot arise simply from the objectionable conduct in question.

What, then, are these pre-existing relationships which might give rise to an obligation of fair dealing beyond the aloofness of the common law? The most important category is fiduciary relationships. Although this is a complex area of the law, it is possible to distinguish between relationships which involve such an expectation of fairness and confidence that the courts, over the years, have been willing to recognise that they justify the obligations of fiduciary trust, and other relationships, which the courts, in considering all the facts and, in particular, the conduct of the dominant party, may find a fiduciary relationship.[18] Thus, where a solicitor[19] (in certain circumstances) or a broker[20] deals with his clients, the courts will assume a fiduciary relationship between the parties and, therefore, an obligation of fair dealing involving a duty of frank disclosure will arise. However, it has long been the law that there is no such relationship between a director of a company and one of the company's shareholders,[21] nor an investor who, by virtue of the investment transaction, becomes a shareholder. A director owes no fiduciary duties, by virtue of being a director, to the shareholders of the company, individually or collectively. The fiduciary obligations which he has are solely to the company which, in law, is an entirely separate legal person from those who own it. However, this is not to say that a director or, for that matter, anyone else, cannot step into a fiduciary relationship with someone who happens to be a shareholder or investor, by virtue of special factors.[22] For example, in the New Zealand case of *Coleman v Myers*[23], the Court of Appeal of New Zealand found that certain dominant directors had stepped into what was, to all intents and purposes, a fiduciary relationship with certain shareholders, and this imposed upon them not only a duty to disclose and not to take personal advantage of price-sensitive, inside information in their dealings with those shareholders, but also a duty of care to the shareholders. In this case, whilst the court was reluctant to formulate a comprehensive test which could be applied in order to impose such exacting duties, it admitted that it was influenced by the fact that the company was closely held, the dependence of the shareholders on the insiders for information relating to the company, the importance that the insiders clearly attached to that information, the significance of the transaction to the parties and the self-interest of the insiders.[24] There are other cases which have recognised that in small companies it may be appropriate to liken shareholders (and even directors) to partners, between which there are obligations of fair dealings.[25]

Avoidance of contracts for illegality (CJA 1993, s 62(2))

Section 62(2) of the Criminal Justice Act 1993 (CJA 1993) provides that 'no contract shall be void or unenforceable by reason only' that it violates s 51. The purpose of this provision, according to the Treasury, is to avoid the difficulties which are associated with undoing deals on a contemporary market. It would seem that the intention behind this provision is to exclude the application of the common law doctrine of illegality. Where the performance of a contract involves the commission of a crime or other act regarded as against public policy, the law will consider the contract void and unenforceable.[26] The previous provision in the Company Securities (Insider Dealing) Act 1986[27] arguably went further than s 62(2) of the CJA 1993, by providing that such a transaction would not be 'void or voidable'. It remains to be seen whether an objectionable contract might be 'avoided' if not void ab initio. Where a contract may be avoided it remains a valid and enforceable contract prior to the initiation of rescission. The point to note, however, is that s 62(2), whilst it may address illegality and the law of mistake, does not rule out an innocent party, in such a transaction, who is seeking to avoid a deal with an insider on some other basis. The most likely justification for seeking rescission would be on the basis of misrepresentation.[28] As has been seen, mere non-disclosure of material information is unlikely to constitute a misrepresentation, but at least s 62(2) appears to leave the door open. It should be noted that under s 2(2) of the Misrepresentation Act 1967 the court has a discretion to refuse rescission, and award damages in lieu thereof, in the case of a non-fraudulent misrepresentation. This would address the concern of the Treasury in regard to unscrambling complicated inter-transaction.

It may be possible for an innocent party dealing with an insider to contend that an objectionable transaction should not be enforced or should be considered void on the wider basis that insider trading is against public policy.[29] It is clear that, without s 62(2) of the CJA 1993, the courts would have no difficulty in striking down contracts which resulted from the commission of an insider trading offence. This much is apparent from the comments of Knox J in *Chase Manhattan Equities v Goodman*.[30] It is arguable that the abuse of privileged information should be regarded as objectionable, whether it falls within s 51 of the CJA 1993 or not. Indeed, it could be argued that there is a broad rule of public policy that such transactions should not be enforced and, thus, the application of the principles of illegality do not operate simply upon the existence of a specific offence under s 51. Knox J was sympathetic to this view in the *Goodman* case,[31] although Kaplan J, in the Hong Kong case of *Innovisions Ltd v Chan Sing-chuk, Charles and Others*,[32] was reluctant to invoke such a general approach to insider trading and thought that it was debatable whether the iniquity of such conduct was such as to 'shock the ordinary citizen or affect the public conscience'. Whilst the Court of Appeal[33] of Hong Kong agreed with Kaplan J on this point, Nazareth JA strongly dissented and took the view that it was open to the courts to consider the application of the law relating to illegality on the basis that insider dealing, whether specifically an offence or not, was contrary to public policy. The authors are inclined to the view of Nazareth JA.

In *Chase Manhattan Equities v Goodman*,[34] Knox J, whilst accepting that the almost identical provision to s 62(2) in the previous law ruled out civil consequences which might otherwise arise from the commission of an insider trading offence, refused to make available the powers of the court to enforce a transaction which was still incomplete, on the basis that to do so would be to enforce an objectionable transaction. The principles of the common law were applied to justify the court in refusing to lend its support to the enforcement of an executory contract for the purchase of shares when it appeared that the transaction was entered into on the basis of inside information. The refusal of the court to assist in consummating an abusive transaction was outside the statutory provision preserving the validity of such contracts. It remains to be seen, however, whether this approach is now correct, given the slightly different wording of s 62(2) of the CJA 1993. The old provision referred to the transaction not being 'void or voidable' by reason of an offence under the statute, whereas s 62(2) refers to a contract not being 'void or unenforceable'. It is arguable that a court could not now decline to enforce such a transaction on the grounds of illegality, given the specific reference to enforceability.

Secret profits

It is a time-honoured principle of fiduciary law that 'a person in a fiduciary position . . . is not, unless otherwise expressly authorised, entitled to make a profit; he is not allowed to put himself in a position where his interest and duty conflict'.[35] Thus, where an insider is in a fiduciary relationship he will not be allowed to derive a secret or unauthorised profit from or through this relationship and, if he does so, he will be bound to yield it up to his principal. It is likely that the profits made from insider dealing would, at least in some cases, be regarded as a secret profit, provided that the opportunity to exploit such privileged information arose by virtue of a fiduciary relationship.[36] However, not every case of insider abuse will involve the exploitation of a fiduciary relationship. It has been seen that there are only certain circumstances in which the courts are prepared to hold persons subject to such onerous obligations of fair dealing. Therefore, whilst a director of a company will be in a fiduciary relationship with his company, he will not be in such a relationship with any other company in the group[37] or with shareholders of the company.[38] There are cases which indicate clearly that if a director utilises in any unauthorised price-sensitive information which comes into his possession by virtue of his office, he will be accountable to his company for the profits which he makes. This is a personal obligation giving rise to personal liability. It would seem that he will not be so liable if he allows another to profit by using the information and does not himself profit.[39] Furthermore, as the rule relates only to the making of secret or unauthorised profits, it probably does not attach to the 'negative profit' made in avoiding a loss, eg by using inside information to sell out before incurring an inevitable loss.[40] In the case of directors, it is also important to note that there will only be liability if the taking of the profit is not properly authorised or has not been excused by the appropriate organ of the company (normally the board of directors). As this liability is to the company and to no one else, it follows that it is only the company which can enforce the obligation on the director to account. There are many difficulties associated with such actions and it is doubtful whether, in the absence of fraud, a minority shareholder could enforce this liability in the face of opposition from the board of directors.[41] It would seem certain that such an action could not be brought, for example, where the matter has been properly put to the shareholders in a general meeting and they have declined to initiate action.[42] Conversely, it is important to remember that this form of liability is not dependent on the company suffering loss or damage. This is because the courts take the view that where a person in a position of confidence abuses his position, this violation of the strict obligations of stewardship is sufficient for liability. The point is underlined by the fact that this view will be taken even where the company is not the issuer of the securities in which the insider trading took place. The company which is entitled to expect fair dealing from those in a fiduciary position will be entitled to enforce this obligation. It is irrelevant whether the profit is made through dealings in its securities or those of another.[43]

Officers of a company will also usually be in a fiduciary relationship with the company[44] and employees will be under a duty of fidelity,[45] which involves similar obligations. Shareholders, no matter how significant their interest in the company, will not be fiduciaries of the company simply by virtue of their contractual relationship. Substantial shareholders may come into a special fiduciary relationship with the company by virtue of becoming, for example, underwriters.[46]

It has been suggested that certain problems relating to the application of the so-called 'secret profits rule' may be avoided by focusing on the exploitation of the inside information rather than on the relationship within which the opportunity to exploit the information arose – in other words to see whether the inside information can be attached to its misuse by those who, by virtue of their position or state of knowledge, are considered to be under a duty not to misuse it. In the case of *Nanus Asia Co Inc v Standard Chartered Bank*,[47] the High Court of Hong Kong was prepared to hold that confidential information, obtained in breach of an employee's duty of fidelity, gave rise to a constructive trust over the profits resulting from its use. The Standard Chartered Bank, having acquired knowledge of the circumstances, was under a duty not to assist their customer, who had exploited the information, in disposing of his profit. The courts have been willing to apply such principles[48] not only to those who exploit the information themselves in the knowledge that it has been obtained in breach of an obligation of trust, but to those who, with knowledge, assist 'constructive trustees' in laundering the proceeds of such misconduct.[49] The imposition of a constructive trust on the profits of, for example, insider dealing, has a number of practical advantages over seeking to impose an accounting for profits. First, a constructive trust gives rise to a proprietary claim which allows profits which have been derived from 'misappropriated' property to be traced. Secondly, as has been seen, any person who takes possession of the trust property with knowledge that it was obtained in breach of trust, or who facilitates the laundering of the proceeds of such a breach of trust, will be liable. This allows, in effect, 'tippees' to be subjected to liability. Thirdly, it is likely that a minority shareholder can maintain a derivative action where the company has a claim to the trust property or its proceeds, but which the board and controllers of the company are reluctant to pursue in the name of the company.

Whilst there is no doubt that the imposition of a constructive trust on those responsible for facilitating a breach of trust, thus imposing liability on a personal basis, is attractive, it is necessary for there to be property involved, which can properly be considered trust property. The constructive trust must fix on property or the proceeds of property. There is controversy as to whether information can be considered property. In Hong Kong it has been assumed that information can be a corporate asset,[50] and US law is sufficiently flexible to render most items of inside information subject to the imposition of restitutionary liability.[51] The position in the UK, however, is more ambiguous.[52] It has been argued that, insofar as the information in question was not capable of constituting trust property, the Hong Kong court in *Nanus Asia Co Inc* erred, according to UK law, in contemplating the imposition of a constructive trust on the proceeds of the inside information.[53] It was held, in *Oxford v Moss*, that confidential information is not property for the purposes of the law of theft and cannot, therefore, be stolen.[54] However, it could be argued that certain types of confidential information are protected by the law in a way which is analogous to the protection of property[55] and, thus, are a form of equitable property capable of constituting trust property.[56] Whilst there is much to be said in favour of such an argument in regard to certain types of information, not all items of inside information could be considered to be of this nature. The law of restitution is, however, developing rapidly and the courts have indicated a firm resolve not to allow 'crooks' to escape with their ill-gotten gains. Therefore, it remains open for a 'robust' decision to take UK law into a less technical era.

Breach of confidence

An action for 'breach of confidence'[57] may be brought to protect information which is considered to be confidential and which arises from, or is otherwise held in confidence in a personal, commercial or other relationship. Information which is obtained in the course of employment or in the exercise of a profession, the disclosure of which would harm the legitimate interests of the employer of the client, will be protected by the law. The confidentiality of information will often be protected by express or implied stipulations in contracts of employment. Breach of such obligations will not only give rise to liability for breach of confidence itself but also found a contractual action for damages. In many cases, it will justify summary dismissal from employment.[58]

Prospects of civil remedies

Knox J made the point, in *Chase Manhattan Securities v Goodman*, that the purpose of s 8(3) of the Company Securities (Insider Dealing) Act 1985 was to remove the effect of the doctrine of illegality on the validity of a transaction which amounted to an offence under that Act, rather than to exclude the operation of the common law principles altogether.[59] It may be argued that s 62(2) of the CJA 1993 is, in one respect, narrower than s 8(3) of the 1985 Act, insofar as it does not prevent rescission,[60] but may be wider in that it could prevent a court declining to enforce a transaction that violates s 51 of the CJA 1993.[61] Neither the Company Securities (Insider Dealing) Act 1985 nor the CJA 1993 address the question of civil liability. Accordingly, they do not bring into question the validity of an objectionable transaction. Thus, if it is possible to find a viable cause of action, it would seem there is nothing to inhibit an action for damages or any other order which would not render the contract void or unenforceable. It is difficult to conceive of a viable inter-party cause of action, even in face-to-face transactions, let alone on the anonymous markets. None the less, there are tantalising references in various Governmental statements that such actions have been contemplated,[62] and Mr Anthony Nelson, the Economic Secretary, in Standing Committee on the Criminal Justice Bill, clearly thought that civil liability was a realistic possibility. He specifically stated that 'a civil remedy is available'. He also stated that civil liability 'could be exercised when an individual has demonstrably lost out because someone has "insider dealt" against his interest, and that can be quantified'.[63] It is possible that Mr Nelson was contemplating the award of compensation under the Powers of the Criminal Courts Act 1973[64] after a conviction, rather than a conventional civil cause of action.[65] It has long been argued that there may be a possibility of a statutory tort action for insider abuse,[66] although the better view is that, given the clear intention of Parliament not to provide express civil liability for insider dealing under Part V of the Companies Act 1980 and under the 1985 Insider Dealing Act, it is most unlikely that a court would find such a cause of action.[67] It could be argued that legislative policy may have changed. Civil liability imposed on both the person with whom the insider deals and on the corporate issuer of the relevant securities (or his corporate principal if the dealings are in another company's securities) is not uncommon in other jurisdictions and was contemplated in many of the discussions leading up to the EC Directive on Insider Dealing.[68] Even if the courts were prepared to find that a statute has created a tort, those seeking compensation will need to establish that the harm caused to them is of a nature that the statutory provision was designed to address and that they are within the scope of the protection afforded by the statute. There are problems in applying these basic requirements to cases of insider abuse on anonymous markets. It could be argued that the harm which the law addresses is a loss of confidence in the market as a whole and not the loss which an individual may have suffered through the random matching of his transaction with an insider. Indeed, it could also be argued that as a willing buyer or seller the investor was a volunteer or, in any case, neither relied on any conduct by the insider nor expected, in an attenuated form, to suffer loss as a consequence of the insider being in the market. Suffice it to say here that, even if a court could be persuaded that Parliament did not intend to rule out the implication of a statutory tort, in action for compensation a plaintiff would have to surmount a number of significant legal hurdles. The Minister's view that this could be done is, in the opinion of the authors, unrealistic.

Section 61 of the FSA 1986 gives the Treasury and the Securities and Investments Board (SIB) the power to bring an action seeking an injunction and an order for restitution or compensation, on behalf of someone indemnified, where there has been a breach of the SIB's Conduct of

Business Rules or the rules of a self-regulating organisation (SRO) or a recognised professional body (RPB).[69] It has been suggested that this power could be used in cases of insider abuse, insofar as the various rules prohibit insider dealings. In practice, the SIB has not exhibited a great enthusiasm for using its civil enforcement powers and it is unlikely that it would wish to chance its arm on what many would consider to be a dangerous and difficult venture.[70] The exercise of similar powers in the US by the Securities and Exchange Commission (SEC) has proved to be the most effective weapon that it has in its arsenal. However, there are procedural and other factors, such as costs, which tend to undermine the efficacy of such enforcement in the UK. If an action was brought under s 61 of the FSA in a case of insider trading where the insider has profited by virtue of his misconduct, it would not be necessary, for an injunction to be decreed and/or a restitution order to be made, for evidence to be adduced of specific loss to persons who have dealt with the insider. This avoids many of the conceptual and practical problems which are involved in determining civil liability according to traditional compensatory procedures. The court is also empowered to appoint a receiver to facilitate the identification and attachment of the illicit profits which have been made by the objectionable transaction. It is important to note that this potentially important device is only available for breaches of a specific Conduct of Business Rule and not simply for a violation of the general law relating to insider dealing.

It is somewhat more problematical whether the general action for damages under s 62 of the FSA 1986 is directly relevant to cases of insider dealing. Section 62 gives to private investors[71] a cause of action for loss suffered to them as a consequence of a breach of a Conduct of Business Rule promulgated by the SIB, and SRO or RPB, relating, inter alia, to insider dealing. As we shall see, such rules tend to be of limited scope and application in regard to insider abuse. It is likely that this statutory tort action would have little utility in market transactions given the requirement that the plaintiff must establish that he has suffered a quantifiable loss by virtue of the contravention in question.

NOTES

1　The Jenkins Committee (Company Law Committee) (Cmnd 1749) recommended, in 1962, that a director who exploited inside information should be liable to both his company for any gain and to the person with whom he dealt for any loss (at para 99). The Select Committee on Trade and Industry also recommended civil liability in its report *Company Investigations* in May 1990 (HC 36) at Recommendation 26. Successive governments have pointed to the complexity of stock market transactions as justification for not providing such liability.

2   See, for example, the observations of Lord Lane CJ in *Attorney-General's Reference (No 1 of 1988)* [1989] BCLC 193 at p 198.

3   The Company Law Committee of Justice observed, in its report, *Insider Trading*, in 1972, that civil liability should be confined to direct transactions on moral as well as practical grounds.

4   See Knox J in *Chase Manhattan Equities v Goodman* [1991] BCLC 897 at p 927.

5   The Department of Trade and Industry took the view that as most inside information was confidential, an insider could not be considered dishonest in failing to disclose it, in the context of a prosecution under s 13 of the Prevention of Fraud (Investments) Act 1958; now s 47(1) of the FSA 1986. See B Rider 'The Crime of Insider Trading' (1978) JBL 19 at p 22. See also p 20.

6   See *Bell v Lever Brothers* [1932] AC 161 and *Moorgate Mercantile Co Ltd v Twitchings* [1976] 2 All ER 641.

7   *Financial Services in the United Kingdom* (1985) (Cmnd 9432) at para 3.4.

8   See *Bodger v Nichols* (1873) 28 LT 441 at p 445 and *Ward v Hobbs* [1878] 4 App Cas 13.

9   See *Carter v Boehm* (1766) 3 Burr 1905 at 1909 in regard to insurance.

10 Note, however, the argument in *Chase Manhattan Equities v Goodman* (above) in regard to the impact of The Stock Exchange's Model Code on conduct for securities transactions by directors of listed companies, and the comments of Brightman J in *Gething v Kilner* [1972] 1 All ER 1164 in regard to the impact of the *City Code on Takeovers and Mergers*. Note also the comments of Mahon J in *Coleman v Myers* [1977] 2 NZLR 225, discussed by B Rider (1977) 40 MLR at p 471.

11 See *Banque Financière de la Cité SA v Westgate Insurance Co Ltd* [1990] 1 QB 665, and the Court of Appeal in *Coleman v Myers* [1977] 2 NZLR 298.

12 *Walters v Morgan* (1861) 3 DeGF & J 718 and *Oakes v Turquand* (1867) 2 LT 325 at p 342.

13 *With v O'Flanagan* [1936] Ch 575.

14 See Lord Wilberforce in *Moorgate Mercantile Co Ltd v Twitchings* [1976] 2 All ER 641 at p 645.

15 But see Milner 'Fraudulent Non-disclosure' (1957) 74 SALJ 177 and B Rider and HL Ffrench at (1977) 94 SALJ 437.

16 See *Chase Manhattan Equities v Goodman* (above).

17 In *Chase Manhattan Equities v Goodman* (above) Knox J accepted that the director in question was under a duty to report his dealings to his company pursuant to The Stock Exchange's *Model Code*. Knox J considered, however, that 'there is too long and tenuous a chain of legal obligation between the duty of a director at one end and a market maker in that security at the other end to justify the finding of a duty owed to the latter by the former to speak' (at p 929). However, would not the argument that there is a duty, at least on the company, be stronger in regard to the timely disclosure of information to an ordinary investor?

18 The categories of fiduciary obligation are not closed. See Donaldson J in *English v Dedham Vale Properties Ltd* [1978] 1 WLR 93 and, generally, Law Comm Consultation Paper No 124 *Fiduciary Duties and Regulatory Rules* (HMSO, 1992) at paras 2.3.4 to 2.4.7.

19 *Brown v IRC* [1965] AC 244.

20 Whilst a stockbroker will often be in a fiduciary relationship with his client, not every aspect of his dealings will have a fiduciary quality. See *Christopher Barker & Sons v IRC* [1919] 2 KB 222 and *King v Hutton* [1900] 2 QB 504. Whilst there is a presumption that an agent is a fiduciary, not all agents are. See *Aluminium Industrie Vaassen BV Romalpah Aluminium Ltd* [1976] 1 WLR 676.

21 *Percival v Wright* [1902] 2 Ch 421 and *Kuwait Asia Bank v National Mutual Life Nominees Ltd* [1990] BCLC 868 at p 888, per Lord Lowry. But note the doubts expressed by Mahony JA in *Glandon pty Ltd & Ors v Strata Consolidated pty & Ors*, 15 September 1993, Court of Appeal (NSW) as to the appropriateness of this outdated approach.

22 *Allan v Hyatt* (1914) 30 TLR 444 and *Briess v Woolley* [1954] AC 333.

23 [1977] 2 NZLR 298. See B Rider (1978) 41 MLR 585.

24 The Court of Appeal of New South Wales in *Glandon pty Ltd & Ors v Strata Consolidated pty & Ors*, 15 September 1993, showed a willingness to follow and possibly expand the approach of the Court of Appeal of New Zealand. Mahony JA also stated that the so-called rule in *Percival v Wright* (above) might reflect the morality of a bygone age.

25 See B Rider 'Partnership Law and its impact on Domestic Companies' (1978) 38 CLJ 148 and *Virdi v Abbey Leisure Ltd* [1990] BCLC 342, as a recent illustration.

26 See generally *Euro-Diam Ltd v Bathurst* [1988] 2 All ER 23 and, particularly, Kerr LJ at p 28.

27 Section 8(3) of the Company Securities (Insider Dealing) Act 1985.

28 Damages may be an appropriate remedy under s 2(1) of the Misrepresentation Act 1967, or in the court's discretion as an alternative to rescission under s 2(2) of that Act or in tort.

29 See, for example, Lord Lane CJ in *Attorney-General's Reference (No 1 of 1988)* [1989] BCLC 193, describing insider trading as 'cheating'. Note also the importance which has been attached to protecting and maintaining confidence in the integrity of the markets.

30 [1991] BCLC 897.

31 Knox J observed in *Chase Manhattan Equities v Goodman* (ibid) that 'It does not . . . necessarily follow that because Parliament has said that no transaction is void or voidable by reason only of an infringement of section 1 [of the offences under the Companies Securities (Insider Dealing) Act 1985] therefore such a transaction is not to be regarded as illegal. The illegality is there by operation of law and the provisions of section 8(3) prevent what would otherwise be the consequences that transactions on The Stock Exchange would need to be unwound' (at p 933).

32 [1992] 1 HKLR 71.

33 [1992] 1 HKLR 255.

34 [1991] BCLC 897.

35 *Bray v Ford* [1986] AC 44, per Lord Herschell at p 51.

36 See generally *Regal (Hastings) Ltd v Gulliver* [1942] 1 All ER 378; *Boardman v Phipps* [1967] 2 AC 46; and *Industrial Development Consultants Ltd v Cooley* [1972] 2 All ER 162. See also B Rider *Insider Trading* (Jordans, 1983) at Ch 2.

37 *Lindgren v L & P Estates Ltd* [1968] Ch 572.

38 See n 22 above.

39 In *Regal (Hastings) Ltd v Gulliver* (above) a director who allowed others to benefit through using what amounted to inside information and opportunity, was not liable in the absence of a personal benefit. See also, on this, *Daniels v Daniels* [1978] Ch 406 and B Rider (1978) CLJ 270 at p 285. Goff and Jones *The Law of Restitution* (2nd edn) (Sweet & Maxwell) at p 493 leave open the question whether the 'tipper' is less than honest. But the integrity of the director in *Regal (Hastings) v Gulliver* (above) cannot be taken for granted. See Scott LJ in *Cooper v Luxor (Eastbourne) Ltd* [1939] 4 All ER 411 at p 416.

40 See *Banque Financière de la Cité SA v Westgate Insurance Co Ltd* [1990] 1 QB 665 and B Rider *Insider Trading* (Jordans, 1983) at p 81. But note that the Court of Appeal in *Coleman v Myers* [1977] 2 NZLR 298 did not adopt such a restrictive approach to the availability of financial compensation.

41 See generally *Gore-Browne on Companies* (44th edn) (Jordans) at Ch 28.

42 *Regal (Hastings) Ltd v Gulliver* (above) at p 36.

43 As liability is based on the abuse of fiduciary trust it does not matter how the profit is generated. See *Reading v AG* [1951] AC 597.

44 *Canadian Aero Services Ltd v O'Malley* (1973) 40 DLR 371 at p 381 per Laskin J.

45 Employees who have authority to act for the company as agents are in a fiduciary relationship, as are 'confidential employees' (*Triplex Safety Glass Co v Scorah* [1938] Ch 211; *AG v Guardian Newspapers Ltd (No 2)* [1990] 1 AC 109). But those employees who merely work for their principle without authority to bind him have lesser obligations (*Bell v Lever Bros* [1932] AC 161). However, the general duty of fidelity on all employees would render them liable to the 'secret profits rule' (*Reading v AG* (above) at p 43; *Boston*

Deep Sea Fishing Ice Co v Ansell (1888) 39 ChD 339; *Hivac Ltd v Park Royal Scientific Instruments Ltd* [1946] 1 All ER 350).

46 *Dunford & Elliot Ltd v Johnson & Firth Brown Ltd* [1977] 1 Lloyd's Rep 505.

47 [1990] 1 HKLR 396.

48 See generally Sir John Mummery 'Liability for involvement in breach of Fiduciary Duty' (1992) *Journal of International Planning* 57; and Sir Peter Millett 'Tracing the Proceeds of Fraud' (1991) 107 LQR 71.

49 *Agip (Africa) Ltd v Jackson* [1991] 3 WLR 116, affirming [1989] 3 WLR 1367. On the laundering aspect, see B Rider 'Fei Ch'ien Launderies – The Pursuit of Flying Money' (1992) *Journal of International Planning* 77.

50 *Carrian Investments Ltd (In Liquidation) v Wong Chong-Po* [1986] HKLR 945; and see also *Bell Houses Ltd v City Wall Properties Ltd* [1966] 2 QB 656.

51 See generally Hanbury and Martin *Modern Equity* (14th Edn) (Sweet & Maxwell) at p 296. The development of the 'misappropriation theory' in regard to insider abuse has tended to accentuate this trend.

52 *Re Barney* [1892] 2 Ch 265 at p 272, per Kekewich J.

53 For example, it is debatable whether the profits generated by the use of what has been described as 'inside information' in *Boardman v Phipps* [1967] 2 AC 46 were properly considered trust property on the basis that the relevant information was property belonging to the family trust. See Hanbury and Maudsley *Modern Equity* (14th edn) (Sweet & Maxwell) at p 598; and B Rider 'The Fiduciary and the Frying Pan' (1978) *Conveyancer and Property Lawyer* 114.

54 (1978) 68 Cr App R 183.

55 *Seager v Copydex (No 2)* [1969] 1 WLR 809; and see Hanbury and Maudsley (above) at pp 729 et seq.

56 See n 53 above.

57 See n 55 above.

58 This has been the result of many cases of insider abuse in the UK.

59 [1991] BCLC 897.

60 Section 8(3) of the 1985 Act refers to a transaction not being 'void or voidable' by virtue of breaching the law on insider trading, see p 65.

61 Section 62(2) refers to no transaction being 'void or unenforceable' by virtue of an offence.

62 *Company Investigations* (Cm 1149) (1990) at p 17.

63 Parliamentary Debates, House of Commons, Standing Committee B, 10 June 1993, col 152.

64 As amended by the Criminal Justice Acts 1982 and 1988. Compensation orders should only be made where there is no doubt as to the offenders liability to compensate the victim (*R v Vivian* [1979] 1 WLR 291) as a rapid means of avoiding the expense and delay of a civil action (*R v Inwood* (1975) 60 Cr App R 70). (It would seem, therefore, that the court must be satisfied that the facts would give rise to a viable civil suit.

65 See p 88 in regard to civil penalties.

66 Most discussion has centred on the possibility of such an action in regard to s 13 of the Prevention of Fraud (Investments) Act 1958, now s 47(1) of the FSA 1986. See B Rider 'The Crime of Insider Trading' (1978) JBL 19.

67 See B Rider *Insider Trading* (Jordans, 1983) at p 44.

68 See generally K Hopt and E Wymeersch (eds) *European Insider Dealing* (Butterworths, 1991) at Pt II.

69 See B Rider, C Abrams and E Ferran *CCH Guide to the Financial Services Act 1986* (2nd edn) (CCH) at p 157.

70 See B Rider 'Insider Trading – A Crime of Our Time?' in *Current Legal Problems, Current Developments in Banking and Finance* (Stevens, 1989) at pp 63 et seq.

71 See s 62A of the FSA 1986, and J Pritchard 'Investor Protection Sacrificed: The New Settlement and Section 62' (1933) 13 *Company Lawyer* at p 171.

CONFLICTS OF INTEREST – CHINESE WALLS

If insider dealing is considered an abuse of a relationship, such as that of a director vis à vis his company, it can be seen in terms of a traditional conflict of interest. Insofar as market-orientated theories are now more in vogue,[1] at least in the UK, seeing insider dealing simply in terms of a conflict of interest gives only part of the picture. None the less, there are many aspects of the law relating to conflicts of interest which are relevant to controlling insider abuse.[2]

One of the most controversial issues is how to resolve conflicting duties between a fiduciary and different principals.[3] There are many situations, in the ordinary course of business in the financial services industry, where an intermediary may be faced with conflicting obligations to different clients. For example, in a now rather dated book on the law relating to The Stock Exchange,[4] there is a statement to the effect that a stockbroker who obtains privileged information should not allow this to operate against the interests of his client.[5] An example could be where a merchant bank obtains highly price-sensitive information from a corporate client and is at the same time advising other clients on investments and may even have discretionary control over their investment funds. Should the bank use the price-sensitive information for the benefit of those clients? Is not a fiduciary, such as the merchant bank, under a duty to advance the interests of its clients, or where the information is likely to have a negative impact, seek to protect its clients' interest? On the other hand, is not the bank under a duty of confidentiality to the corporate client. Also the law relating to insider dealing must be considered. Given the host of legal and regulatory problems that surround multiple-function and multiple-client fiduciaries in the UK financial services industry, it is, perhaps, surprising, that more thought has not been given to this topic. It is not proposed here to analyse all the various interplays between fiduciary law, the law of contract and tort, the criminal law, common law illegality and the impact of delegated legislation and the various rules promulgated by the self-regulatory organisations. Indeed, the Law Commission is presently embarked on just this task.[6] Suffice it to say, that the City institutions have long recognised the danger of conflicts of interests and conflicts of duties and have adopted the expedient of the 'Chinese Wall'.[7] This is simply the creation, within an organisation, of physical and operational segregation of functions. Those people engaged in advising companies are separated, in terms of location and work, from those engaged in investment-related functions. Rules and procedures are put in place, with compliance monitoring, to ensure that information does not pass from one function to the other. As we have seen, the expedient of segregation has been endorsed, at least to a limited extent, by the FSA 1986,[8] the SIB[9] and various self-regulatory agencies[10] and is widely adopted throughout the world.[11] However, there remain doubts as to whether segregation of functions and non-communication of information will protect a firm from a civil action brought against it. For example, would it be a good defence to a claim in negligence that those people advising a client were unaware of information, because of a Chinese Wall, which with the exercise of reasonable care they should have had and which would have protected the client's interest? By the same token it is unclear whether Chinese Walls would protect a fiduciary from allegations that he has breached his fundamental obligation to avoid placing himself in a conflict of interest, regardless of how properly he does, in fact, behave. Even the Government has recognised that Chinese Walls restrict the flow of information and do not avoid the existence and, presumably, the consequences of a conflict of interest.[12] Given the importance that courts attach to fiduciary obligations[13] and the notion that 'justice must not only be done, it must clearly be seen to be done',[14] the courts have not been sympathetic to those who have sought to manage conflicts of interest by internal procedures and training. Indeed, judges have doubted whether a person can be trained to act with integrity once they are placed in a conflict situation.[15] Where the Chinese Wall is little more than a 'bamboo' curtain and its integrity cannot be demonstrated, the courts have been most unsympathetic.[16] However, the Privy Council, in a recent case,[17] took a more realistic approach and recognised that if certain aspects of business are not to be rendered impossible, 'there must be an implied term of the contract . . . that he is entitled to act for other principals . . . and to keep confidential the information obtained from each of his principals.'[18]

In another recent Privy Council opinion,[19] the Board held that a solicitor may act for both parties provided he has first obtained 'informed consent' from them. This means consent given in the knowledge that there is a conflict and that consequentially the solicitor may be disabled from disclosing to each party the full knowledge which he possesses or may be disabled from advising one of the parties on a particular matter.

The SIB is of the opinion that a company's compliance with the SIB rules relating to segregation will not only excuse that company from what otherwise might be considered breaches of its Conduct of Business Rules, but will also afford companies protection against civil claims.[20] It is not entirely clear, however, that the SIB's Conduct of Business Rules (let alone those of purely self-regulatory authorities) can, without statutory backing, modify principles of common law and equity.[21] A court would be justified in looking at the Rules and what in fact took place in fashioning the application of these long-established obligations, but it is by no means certain that the general law can be pre-empted. Furthermore, it is not enough simply to assert that now that insider dealing constitutes a specific crime there can be no duty to utilise such information for the benefit of a client at civil law. Criminal liability is confined to individuals and any civil suit would probably be brought against a company and, thus, would be outside the reach of the criminal law. Suffice it to say that because of these and other uncertainties, many have called for specific legislation recognising the efficacy of Chinese Walls.[22] Whilst it would be wrong to try to predict what conclusions the Law Commission will reach at the end of its study, it is not unlikely that it will advocate legislation. It is the Law Commission's provisional view that, without full disclosure to those dealing with an intermediary as to the arrangements which are in operation to prevent the flow and abuse of information, a Chinese Wall may not be effective protection against a civil claim. This is a view which is widely held. Indeed, many would argue that the Chinese Wall would need to be reinforced by 'no recommendation policies' and 'restricted dealing lists'. Governments have not been enthusiastic about seeking to legislate in this area. The previous provisions on insider dealing contained a defence, in s 7 of the Company Securities (Insider Dealing) Act 1985 which enabled a trust to deal, in circumstances where one of the trustees would himself be prohibited from dealing, if the trust acted on the advice of an independent adviser who did not appear to be an insider and, of course, that the inside information was not, in fact, communicated. The SIB Core Rules contain a similar defence for firms. The Government did not consider that a special defence was necessary for trustees under the new law. The reason for this is that 'the Government does not believe that trust law can require trustees to commit a criminal offence'. Of course, this does not necessarily solve all the problems for an intermediary, as we have seen. Indeed, given the arguably wider scope of the new legislation the problems for financial intermediaries are likely to be greater rather than less.[23]

NOTES

1 See p 13.

2 See p 63 et seq.

3 See generally RM Goode (ed) *Conflicts of Interest in the Changing Financial World* (Institute of Bankers, 1986).

4 See G Cooper and R Cridlan *The Law and Procedure of the Stock Exchange* (Butterworths, 1971) at p 104. See also the discussion of *Boardman v Phipps* [1967] 2 AC 46 in B Rider 'The Fiduciary and the Frying Pan' (1978) *Conveyancer and Property Lawyer* 114.

5 In *Kelly v Cooper* [1993] AC 205, Lord Browne-Wilkinson observed 'stockbrokers . . . cannot be contractually bound to disclose to their private clients inside information disclosed to the brokers in confidence by a company for which they also act'.

6 Law Comm Consultation Paper No 124 *Fiduciary Duties and Regulatory Rules* (HMSO, 1992). See also DJ Hayton *Report on Financial Services and Trust Law* (SIB and IMRO, 1990).

7   See generally B Rider 'Conflicts of Interest and Chinese Walls' in B Rider (Ed) *The Regulation of the British Securities Industry* (Oyez, 1979) at Ch 5. See also the Appendix to the *Annual Report 1970 of the City Panel on Takeovers and Mergers.*

8   See s 48(2)(h) of the FSA 1986 and see para 2 of the former Licensed Dealers (Conduct of Business) Rules 1983, SI 1983/585.

9   See Core Rule 34.

10 See generally *CCH Financial Services Reporter* (CCH), Vols 2 and 3.

11 See NS Poser 'Chinese Wall or Emperor's New Clothes?' (1988) 9 *Company Lawyer* 119 and, in particular, *Broker–Dealer Policies and Procedures Designed to Segregate the Flow and Prevent the Misuse of Material Non-Public Information* (SEC, 1990).

12 See *Financial Services in the UK* (Cmnd 9432) (1985).

13 See p 66 et seq.

14 See *Supasave Retail Ltd v Coward Chance* [1991] BCLC 519 and, particularly, the judgment of Sir Nicholas Browne-Wilkinson VC.

15 In *North and South Trust Co v Berkeley* [1971] 1 All ER 980, Donaldson J stated 'how do you train anyone to act properly in such a situation? What course of action can possibly be adopted which does not involve some breach of duty to one principal or the other . . . neither skill nor honesty can reconcile the irreconcilable (at p 991). See also *Anglo–African Merchants Ltd v Bayley* (1969) 1 All ER 421.

16 See n 13 above and also *Re a Firm of Solicitors* [1992] 1 All ER 353.

17 *Kelly v Cooper* (1992) above at n 5.

18 The Law Commission has arguably taken a different view, 'while a firm would not be compelled to disclose or utilise the information . . . the fact that it owes a duty of confidentiality . . . will not constitute a defence to a breach of duty' such as in the law of tort to another, see above at n 6 at 3.4.30.

19 *Clark Boyce v Mouat* [1993] 4 All ER 268.

20 See p 79 et seq.

21 See n 5 above and *Fiduciary Duties and Regulatory Rules, The Law Society's Response* (Law Society, 1992) and *Fiduciary Duties and Regulatory Rules – the Implications for the Financial Services Industry* (Clifford Chance, 1992).

22 See B Rider 'Conflicts of Interest and Chinese Walls' (above) at pp 98 et seq for the various legislative proposals prior to the Companies Act 1980.

23 *The Law on Insider Dealing: A Consultative Document* (DTI, 1989) at p 17.

SELF-REGULATION AND COMPLIANCE

Whilst it would be somewhat misleading to think in terms of the system of supervision and control over the financial markets prior to 1986 being wholly self-regulatory in character, it is true that, in large measure, the only rules which had effect were non-statutory.[1] Considerable reliance was placed on the efficacy of self-regulatory procedures. In regard to insider dealing, these ranged from the very developed obligations of the *City Code on Takeovers and Mergers*[2] and the Model Code on conduct for securities transactions by directors of listed companies (the *Model Code*),[3] at one end of the scale, to the vague, albeit worthy, edicts of the less well-organised City institutions at the other end. However, by 1973, even the Panel on Takeovers and Mergers and The Stock Exchange, which were much better placed than most to make self-regulation work through controlling access to the privileges of the market, recognised that legislation was required and called for insider dealing to be made a specific criminal offence.[4] When insider dealing was criminalised in 1980, this shifted the burden of enforcement from the City bodies to Government. Self-regulatory authorities remained concerned to discourage and detect abuse, but were justifiably concerned not to become involved in legal proceedings.[5] The FSA 1986, whilst continuing self-regulation as an essential and pervading element in the new regulatory structure, passed back to the revamped self-regulators the primary responsibility for policing their members. The new regime gave them the responsibility for ensuring adequate compliance, by their members, with the law and, in particular, with the standards set by the SIB for the conduct of investment business.[6] Whilst many of these standards have a bearing on fair dealing and probity, the SIB has always required observance of the law on insider dealing. Core Rule 28(2) places an obligation on firms to use their best endeavours to ensure that they do not knowingly effect, either in the course of regulated business or otherwise, a transaction for a customer which it knows is prohibited by s 51 of CJA 1993. This is an important provision as it places an obligation on firms to take care that they do not facilitate the execution of transactions for their customers which would constitute insider dealing. In other words, firms are under a positive duty not to transact business for a person who they know is committing an offence. If they do not know the circumstances, and the Chinese Wall defence operates in such cases, there is no breach of the Core Rule. Firms are under no duty to question their clients and ascertain whether a transaction is objectionable. In order for the Rules to apply they must actually know that the transaction is objectionable. Presumably, to 'know', in this context, would include deliberately shutting one's eyes to the obvious. This is, however, to be judged on a subjective basis and it would have to be proved that those responsible did actually know the facts. Proof that any reasonable person in their position would have known may raise an inference, but would not, in itself, establish knowledge.[7]

Core Rule 29(1) and (2) will not apply, however, where the inside information is the firm's own intentions. This is necessary because otherwise knowledge within the firm that it was to take a particular position would preclude it from taking that position. Core Rule 28(3)(b) also excludes from the operation of the obligations imposed under Core Rule 29(1) and (2) a firm which is a recognised market maker which is under an obligation to deal in the relevant securities. This is to enable a market maker which has been duly recognised by an investment exchange to maintain its proper function in the market by ensuring stability and liquidity. Finally, Core Rule 29(c) also excludes a firm where it is a trustee or personal representative, provided that it acts on the advice of a third party appearing to be an appropriate adviser who is not prohibited from dealing. This provision corresponded with s 7(1) of the Company Securities (Insider Dealing) Act 1985 and it remains to be seen whether it is now appropriate under the new law.[8]

Whilst the SIB and each self-regulatory organisation and recognised professional body has its own rule book, a degree of cohesion has been achieved by virtue of, what is described as, the 'New settlement', which was brought about by amendments introduced by the Companies Act 1989.[9] There are now three tiers of Conduct of Business Rules which apply to all those who conduct investment business in the UK, whether they are authorised directly by the SIB or by one of the self-regulatory authorities or, for that matter, if they have not bothered to seek authorisation. The first tier consists of 10 General Principles, which, as we shall see, are of little practical significance in combating insider abuse. The second, and most important tier consists of a series of Core Rules promulgated by the SIB for general application throughout the industry. The third tier consists of rules and codes which flesh out the Core Rules and provide for specific regulation within the relevant areas of activity. Thus, there is some variation in the rules of the self-regulatory authorities in this third tier and, in cases of so-called 'derogations', there is some variation even in regard to the Core Rules. However, for present purposes it is enough to concentrate on the Core Rules[10] and, in particular, the Rule which specifically addresses the problem of insider dealing.

Core Rule 28(1) provides that 'a firm must not effect (either in the UK or elsewhere) an own account transaction when it knows of circumstances which mean that it, its associate, or an employee of either, is prohibited from effecting that transaction by the statutory restrictions on insider dealing'. The General Counsel[11] to the SIB considers that this Rule provides an important civil law supplement to the criminal provisions. First, it makes it clear that a firm can be liable, whereas the criminal offences only apply to individuals.[12] Furthermore, a breach of the Core Rules may give rise to civil liability under ss 61 and 62 of the FSA 1986, as we have seen.[13] It is important to note, however, that a firm will only be liable for a breach of Core Rule 28(1) if it is aware that someone connected with it cannot deal by virtue of the CJA 1993, s 51. Core Rule 36(3) provides that a firm will only be taken to have acted knowingly if the individuals who act on behalf of the firm act with knowledge. Thus, if there is an effective Chinese Wall in place, so that those who happen to deal in the relevant securities are unaware that one of their colleagues is prohibited from dealing, the firm will not have violated Core Rule 28(1). It is only where an associate of the firm, the firm itself, or an employee of either is actually within the scope of the CJA 1993, s 51, that Core Rule 36(3) comes into play in any case. Associates, in this context, include individuals appointed as representatives of the firm, or any other person whose business or domestic relationship with the firm or, for that matter, another associate, could reasonably be expected to give rise to a community of interest between them which may involve a conflict of interest in dealings with third parties.[14] The SIB takes the view that conduct on the part of a firm which is outside the scope of a Core Rule, such as Core Rule 28, might still be considered objectionable under the SIB's General Principles. In particular, General Principle 1 states that 'a firm should observe high standards of integrity and fair dealing'. Furthermore, General Principle 3 places firms under an obligation to comply with good market practices and to such codes and other standards which have been endorsed by the SIB. Thus, the *City Code on Takeovers and Mergers*[15] and the *Model Code*, would be considered binding on firms. However, it must be noted that non-compliance with the SIB's General Principles, whilst possibly giving rise to disciplinary action on the part of the SIB, have no legal consequences under ss 61 and 62 of the FSA 1986.[16]

Compliance, or in-house regulation as it used to be called,[17] has become very much more important in recent years and especially since the creation of the new regulatory structure under the FSA 1986. Although The Stock Exchange and, to a lesser extent, the Panel on Takeovers and Mergers,[18] required compliance procedures to be drawn up and applied, there were few uniform standards, until recently, in those procedures or in the way in which they were applied. Even today, research indicates widely different views among compliance officers on their roles and on whether they are actually performing a 'policing' function.[19] The structure of regulation imposed on the financial services industry by the FSA 1986 places considerable emphasis on authorised firms having in place adequate in-house procedures for preventing and controlling abusive and improper practices and in providing adequate resources to properly monitor and enforce these rules. Self-regulatory authorities are bound, as a condition of being 'recognised' by the SIB, to ensure that their members have, and operate, adequate compliance procedures. The FSA 1986 places an obligation, in turn, on the SIB to ensure that the recognised self-regulatory authorities discharge this supervisory function. Although it is widely argued that there is nothing new in these compliance procedures, the systems and resources which must be in place today bear little resemblance to the vague and unrefined codes and procedures of the past, which were policed by avuncular semi-retired partners or timorous clerks. On the other hand, it is still the case that some compliance officers feel under pressure to contribute more to the fortune of their employer's enterprise than ensuring that their employer remains inside the law! The role of compliance officers as internal monitors (let alone reluctant and untrained policemen) is a confusing one and has yet to settle down in the UK financial services industry.[20]

Core Rule 34 requires authorised firms to take reasonable steps, including the maintenance of procedures, to ensure that their officers and employees, and officers and employees of their appointed representatives, comply with the responsibilities which the law, particularly the law relating to insider dealing, places upon their employers. Moreover, these procedures must also address the 'propriety of personal dealings' and place an obligation on those concerned to report their dealings and interests to the employer, where such information must be properly recorded. There is some variation in the manner of implementation of these provisions within the various jurisdictions of the self-regulatory authorities.[21] The Investment Management Regulatory Organisation (IMRO),[22] for example, in Rule 1.5(2) of the IMRO Rules, provides that each member must take reasonable steps to ensure that none of its officers or employees or those of its appointed representatives, either on his own account or that of any connected person,[23] effects any transaction which, among other things, is an investment at a time when he knows or should reasonably know that this would contravene the law on insider dealing. The procedures operated by member firms generally involve: (a) the prior approval of certain transactions by a designated official; (b) the prohibition of all dealings in certain securities or at certain times; (c) the recording of transactions; and (d) the preservation of confidentiality. The new regulatory regime places an obligation on authorised firms, as employers, to ensure that their employees act properly and, in many respects, this is not simply an obligation borne out of the fear of being sued vicariously for their misconduct. Therefore, it is now common to find contracts of employment incorporating, directly or by reference, the obligations imposed on officers and employees under such compliance procedures.[24] In many respects, the obligations of an authorised person to ensure proper compliance are even greater in relation to appointed representatives, who are not themselves authorised and are 'regulated' through the principal relationship.[25]

The Stock Exchange first published a Model Code on conduct for securities transactions by directors of listed companies in 1977,[26] which set out a minimum standard of good practice against which listed companies could measure and refine their own internal compliance procedures. The Listing Rules impose upon listed issuers a contractual obligation to ensure that they operate rules no less demanding than those contained in the *Model Code*. As Knox J stated, in *Chase Manhattan Securities v Goodman*,[27] the obligation to operate such procedures is placed on the company and not on individual directors of the company. It was contended in that case, however, that a director who failed to report dealings to his company, as he was bound to pursuant to the *Model Code*, in effect represented in the transaction that he was not an insider of the company under such a duty. Knox J recognised that a duty to speak to one person, here the company, might give rise to liability to a third person. In that case the contention that breach of the *Code* constituted a misrepresentation to the market was held to be untenable.[28] It is interesting, however, that Knox J clearly thought that the director in question was under an obligation to comply with the *Model Code*, as he was aware of its terms, even though there was no evidence that his company had incorporated the *Model Code* into any contract with him. It remains to be seen whether, according to this view, a breach of the terms of the *Model Code*, even if it has not been incorporated into a contract, would give rise to a claim in damages – although it would presumably justify dismissal.

The *Model Code* emphasises that there is no objection to a director investing in the securities of his own company. However, he must always comply with the law relating to insider dealing[29] and notify an appointed director, or the board of directors, prior to any dealings in the securities of his company.[30] The *Model Code* extends the prohibitions on dealing contained in the CJA 1993 to what are termed 'close periods' where, although he may not be guilty of an offence, it would be imprudent for a director of a listed company to deal. The *Model Code* prohibits a director from dealing in the securities of his own company or in the securities of another listed company, if he is in possession of unpublished, price-sensitive information. It should be noted that when a director deals in the securities of his company the prohibition will apply irrespective of how he came into possession of the information, although where the trading is in the securities of another issuer it seems that the director must have acquired the relevant information by virtue of being a director of his company. Whilst The Stock Exchange has, in the past, been reluctant to define unpublished, price-sensitive information, it has now adopted the formula in s 10 of the Company Securities (Insider Dealing) Act 1985.[32] The *Model Code* is applicable to dealings by or on behalf of a director's spouse or infant child. Unlike the CJA 1993, the *Model Code* does not apply to foreign companies. Furthermore, it should be noted that the *Model Code* makes it clear that it applies in full force even where a director places his investments under discretionary professional management. Whilst the *Model*

Code only applies to directors and their families, boards are encouraged to apply the same standards to relevant employees.

NOTES

1   See generally B Rider (Ed) *The Regulation of the British Securities Industry* (Oyez, 1979) at Chs 1 and 2.
2   B Rider 'Self-regulation: The British approach to policing conduct in the securities business, with particular reference to the role of the City panel on Takeovers and Mergers in the regulation of insider trading' (1978) 1 *Journal of Comparative Corporate Law and Securities Regulation* 319.
3   Now called the *Model Code* and appearing in the Appendix to Chapter 16 of *The Listing Rules* (see App 3).
4   For the history of insider dealing regulation in Britain prior to Part V of the Companies Act 1980 see B Rider and HL Ffrench *The Regulation of Insider Trading* (Macmillan, 1979) at Ch 6.
5   See generally B Rider *Insider Trading* (Jordans, 1983) at Ch 3.
6   On the regulatory structure, see J Suter *The Regulation of Insider Dealing in Britain* (Butterworths, 1989) at Ch 2 and B Rider, C Abrams and E Ferran *CCH Guide to the Financial Services Act 1986* (2nd edn) (CCH), at Ch 3.
7   This is referred to by Professor David Hayton as 'Nelsonian' knowledge – obtainable but for deliberately shutting one's eyes to the obvious (DJ Hayton *The Law of Trusts* (2nd edn) (Sweet & Maxwell, 1993) at p 20).
8   See p 54.
9   See M Blair *Financial Services – The New Rules* (Blackstone, 1991) and J Pritchard 'Investor Protection Sacrificed: The New Settlement' (1992) 13 *Company Lawyer* 171.
10 For all the Rule Books see *CCH Financial Services Reporter* (CCH), Vols 2 and 3.
11 See M Blair *Financial Services – The New Rules* (above).
12 See p 22.
13 See p 70 et seq.
14 See M Blair *Financial Services – The New Rules* (above).
15 There are a number of provisions in the *City Code on Takeovers and Mergers* which impinge on insider dealing. The substantive prohibition is in Rule 4, but there are rules relating to the disclosure and reporting of transactions and timely disclosure of relevant information. See generally M Ashe and L Counsell *Insider Trading* (Fourmat, 1990) at pp 99 et seq.
16 Note also the *International Conduct of Business Principles* promulgated by the International Organisation of Securities Commissions (IOSCO, 1991), which have been endorsed by the SIB and which emphasise the importance of fair dealing and avoidance of conflicts of interest. It does not specifically refer to insider dealing. In practice, it is likely to be of even less significance than the *European Code of Conduct Relating to Transactions in Transferable Securities* OJ 20 August 1977 L212/37.
17 See n 4 above.
18 See n 6 above.
19 Note the particularly valuable work of Rowan Bosworth-Davies in this regard in *An Examination of the Attitudes of Financial Services Compliance Officers to the Criminal Offence of Insider Dealing* (1993) MA Dissertation, University of Exeter.
20 Rowan Bosworth-Davies' research supports earlier studies which suggest that compliance officers do not consider insider dealing a particularly serious problem, both in terms of its incidence and criminality. However, see also M Weait 'The Contribution of

the Compliance Function of Effective Financial Services Regulation' (1993) *Journal of Asset Protection and Financial Crime* 83.

21 See generally *CCH Financial Securities Reporter* (CCH), Vols 2 and 3.

22 IMRO Rules 8–234, Release 19:10–i–92.

23 'Connected person' is defined in the IMRO Rules to mean anyone connected with the officer or employee concerned, by reason of a domestic or business relationship (other than those which arise solely because that person is a customer of the member), such that the officer or employee has influence over that person's judgment as to how to invest his property or exercise any rights attaching to his investments.

24 There have been several examples of officers and employees being dismissed for violating in-house compliance procedures. See J Suter *The Regulation of Insider Dealing in Britain* (Butterworths, 1989) at p 286.

25 In the US, by virtue of s 21A(a)(3) of the Securities Exchange Act 1934, as amended, controlling persons, who would include the employing firm of those working within the financial services industry, are liable to civil penalties based on multiples of the employee's profit, provided that the controller 'knew or recklessly disregarded the fact that the controlled person was likely to engage' in insider dealing, by trading or tipping, and 'failed to take appropriate steps to prevent such acts'. Thus, without a suitable compliance system, firms will find it almost impossible to escape what could prove to be a very significant financial penalty.

26 See M Ashe and L Counsell *Insider Trading* (Fourmat, 1990) at p 110.

27 [1991] BCLC 897 at p 924.

28 Ibid, at 929.

29 *Model Code*, Rule 4.

30 Ibid, Rule 6.

31 Ibid, Rule 3.

32 Ibid, Rule 1(f) with the assumption that any information regarding transactions required to be notified to the Company Announcements Office under Chapters 10 and 11 of *The Listing Rules* is price sensitive.

INVESTIGATION AND ENFORCEMENT

It has long been recognised in the UK that the investigation and prosecution of crime in the financial sector presents problems of a particularly
difficult nature. The Royal Commission appointed to inquire into the
regulation of The Stock Exchange in 1878, under the chairmanship of Lord
Penzance,[1] noted these problems and advocated the appointment of a
particular public official to ensure proper prosecution of cases of fraud. It
took over 100 years and several more such recommendations[2] before the
creation of the Serious Fraud Office under the Criminal Justice Act 1987.[3]
Discussion of the problems associated with the detection, pursuit and
prosecution of 'white collar' crime will not be discussed here. It is enough
to point out that most countries have encountered very serious problems
in adequately combating insider abuse through the ordinary criminal
justice system.[4] Whilst the record of the authorities in the UK has not, by
international standards, been bad, given the vast amount of suspected
instances of abuse the conviction record is not impressive.[5] It could be that
those cases which are detected are not susceptible to the degree of inquiry
which is necessary for an effective criminal prosecution. It cannot be
supposed that every unusual and unexplained transaction identified by
The Stock Exchange's Insider Dealing Group[6] is, in fact, a case of insider
dealing which would properly fall within the relevant offence. It is the case,
however, that many people in the self-regulatory tier of supervision feel
that the Department of Trade and Industry, and now the Treasury, have
been reluctant to pursue cases with the vigour and resources that may be
required to secure more convictions. On the other hand, the costs involved
in pursuing such cases and the practical problems involved in bringing a
case to court should not be underestimated.[7] Given the ease with which
nominees, especially those out of the jurisdiction, and financial intermediaries can be utilised to obscure ownership and confuse investigators, those
who are prepared to apply a modicum of thought and planning to their
unsocial activities can frustrate most regulatory mechanisms.[8]

When insider dealing was first made a specific criminal offence under
Part V of the Companies Act 1980, the Government rejected calls to
provide those charged with enforcing the new provisions with additional
powers of investigation. Unfortunately, given the number of serious
scandals which came to light involving sophisticated insider dealing syndi-
cates, the Government was forced to reconsider its position, and s 177 of
the FSA 1986 confers a 'new' power on the Secretary of State to investigate
insider dealing offences. The powers provided for in this section are very
similar to those which already existed in the Companies Act 1985 for
investigating the affairs of companies and the beneficial ownership of

shares. Under s 177(1), if it appears to the Economic Secretary that there are circumstances suggesting that there have been violations of s 51 of the CJA 1993, he may appoint one or more inspectors to carry out 'such investigations as are requisite to establish whether or not any such contravention has occurred' and to report the results to him. If the inspectors consider that any person can or may be able to give information concerning any such offence, they may require that person to produce any documents in his possession or control relating to the issuer of the relevant securities or its securities, to attend before them and to give them all other assistance which 'he is reasonably able to give' in regard to the investigation. Inspectors may administer oaths and examine any such person under oath. A statement made by a person in compliance with a request made under s 177 can be used in evidence against him. Section 178 of the FSA 1986 provides important sanctions to be employed against those who fail to co-operate with inspectors appointed under s 177. Section 178(2) provides that where there is a refusal to co-operate, the inspectors are empowered to certify this to the court, and the court is empowered to inquire into the matter. If, after hearing evidence from both parties, the court is of the opinion that the refusal to co-operate is unreasonable, it may punish the person concerned as if he stood guilty of contempt.[9]

In addition to punishing the person who unreasonably refuses to co-operate with the inspectors as a matter of contempt, the court may direct that the Treasury may use far-ranging regulatory and disciplinary powers under s 178(2)(b) of the FSA 1986. It is also provided, in 178(2), that the court may make such a direction, notwithstanding that the person concerned is not within the jurisdiction, if the court is satisfied that he was notified of his right to appear before the court and of the court's powers under this section.

Section 178(6) of the FSA 1986 provides that a person who is asked to provide information or furnish a document shall not be taken to have a reasonable excuse for refusing to co-operate where the suspected offence relates to dealing by him on the instructions of, or for the account of, another person, simply because at the time of his refusal he did not know the identity of that other person; nor is it a reasonable excuse that he was subject to the law of another jurisdiction prohibiting him from disclosing information relating to that transaction without the consent of that other person, if he might have obtained that consent or obtained exemption from that law.

The practical importance of effective, international co-operation in policing insider dealing abuse has been dramatically underlined in a number of recent cases. The UK Government, in addition to making insider dealing an extraditable offence under the Criminal Justice Act 1988, and signing the Council of Europe Convention on Insider Dealing, has entered into a number of bilateral agreements with foreign governments through the Department of Trade and Industry and the Treasury, under which it is permissible for regulatory authorities to exchange information and intelligence in the area of corporate securities regulation and, specifically, insider trading.[10] Sections 82 and 83 of the Companies Act 1989 allow the Treasury and the Department of Trade and Industry to respond to requests for assistance from foreign regulatory authorities by utilising their statutory powers of investigation. The UK Government's ability to co-operate with other member states in fighting such abuses as insider dealing has also been enhanced by the Criminal Justice (International Co-operation) Act 1990.[11]

In the US the vast majority of cases of insider dealing do not result in a criminal prosecution. The SEC, under the US Constitution, does not have the authority to prosecute criminal cases, as this is the preserve of the US Department of Justice. The SEC has, however, in the case of insider dealing since 1960, fashioned and developed an important civil enforcement jurisdiction.[12] The SEC brings actions before the Federal Courts seeking the imposition of an injunction on the wrong-doer and, attached to this order, it often seeks other decrees, such as the mandatory 'disgorgement' of profits or the imposition of an agreed system of internal compliance. Indeed, given the nature of civil proceedings in the US and the rather different approach of US courts to the issue of costs, most defendants 'agree' with the SEC on the imposition of a 'consent order', in which the defendant will accept the terms of the decree without necessarily admitting his guilt. Thus, he will be enjoined from future violations, giving the SEC the right to bring him before the courts for contempt if a further violation occurs. The civil enforcement jurisdiction of the SEC has been so impressive, in relative terms, that the US Congress has given the SEC the power to impose civil penalties.[13] It has been argued in the UK, not least by the authors,[14] that this approach is likely to be more effective, and should be introduced here. The authors do not contend that the imposition of civil penalties or restitutionary liability should necessarily replace the criminal law – as in the USA, where the SEC keeps the 'shotgun behind the door' (namely a criminal referral) for particularly egregious cases. Furthermore, whilst there are certain practical advantages in pursuing a wrongdoer through the civil courts in other countries, as the *Nanus Asia Inc* case[15] clearly showed, most systems and procedures for international mutual assistance depend, to a greater or lesser extent, on the conduct in question being capable of constituting a specific criminal offence.[16]

Whilst the authors accept that there is no panacea for dealing with insider dealing or, for that matter, any species of economic crime, they are of the view that the criminal justice system, despite all the efforts of the present Government to improve it,[17] cannot be expected to 'bring the perpetrators of serious fraud' (let alone insider dealing) 'expeditiously and effectively to book'.[18] It may be that the 'juggernaut' of the criminal law will occasionally drag the insider before the courts but, at the end of the day, if it is important to promote confidence in the integrity of the financial markets it is desirable to have in place procedures which can be expected, both by society and the 'crooks', to be more effective and efficient. Resort to civil enforcement procedures, along the lines of those in the US, would be, in all probability, quicker, cheaper and more efficacious. The authors have also proposed the creation, by statute, of a civil cause of action by the issuer of the relevant securities against anyone guilty of engaging in what would constitute, in a criminal prosecution, an offence under the CJA 1993.[19] The House of Commons' Select Committee on Trade and Industry, in its *Report on Company Investigations*, considered that there was considerable merit in these proposals and recommended that the Government give thought to developing a viable civil enforcement regime.[20] However, this was rejected by the Department of Trade and Industry,[21] on the basis that insider dealing constituted a wrong against the public and 'this is the classical reason for creating a criminal offence – such as murder or theft'. This is a rather naive approach, as there are other areas of the law, such as taxation, where civil penalties are employed to give effect to a public purpose, and history shows numerous instances where the civil law was used to reinforce and give effect to the criminal law. Given the controversy which has continued to surround the enforcement of insider dealing law, in recent months both the SIB and the Serious Fraud Office have expressed support for the development of civil and administrative enforcement in this area. It remains to be seen whether the Government will rethink its approach. There would be nothing contrary to such an approach in the EC Directive on Insider Dealing, as it leaves open to member states the determination of suitable penalties. Article 13 of the Directive merely states that 'penalties shall be sufficient to promote compliance'. Most European countries have both a criminal and an administrative enforcement regime.

Section 60(2) of the CJA 1993 provides that no prosecution for an offence under the insider dealing provisions shall be brought without the consent, in England and Wales, of either the Treasury or the Director of Public Prosecutions. In Scotland, prosecutions are brought by the Lord Advocate. The restriction on commencing prosecutions for insider dealing was first introduced in 1980 to prevent vexatious and trivial cases. The Companies Act 1989 amended the law, which had previously provided that the prosecution had to be brought by the Department of Trade and Industry or the Director of Public Prosecutions to enable permission to be given to other prosecutorial authorities. Since 1989, the Insider Dealing Group of The Stock Exchange has been permitted to bring prosecutions. Given the private status of The Stock Exchange, this has raised the eyebrows of foreign commentators, albeit that few in the UK appear to have noticed. The Serious Fraud Office (SFO), which has wide-ranging inquisitorial powers under s 2 of the Criminal Justice Act 1987[22] and facilities for international co-operation, might be thought to be ideally placed to take on the prosecution of what has proved to be a difficult crime to deal with within the traditional criminal justice system, has been un-enthusiastic. Indeed, it was the view of the SFO that insider dealing, on its own, was unlikely to rank as a 'serious or complex fraud' so as to justify resort to its powers and resources.[23] Whether such a view is still current within the SFO is unknown, although it is true that, somewhat bloodied by a series of unfortunate cases involving the financial markets, the present Director has expressed the view that many such matters would be far more effectively and efficiently (both in political and economic terms) dealt with by the City regulatory bodies themselves, as essentially disciplinary matters.[24]

The courts, whilst speaking out against insider abuse, have not always found themselves in a position to apply penalties which would appear, to the man in the street, as likely to discourage those concerned from 'chancing their hand' in the future. The approach in the US has been to make sure that, at a minimum, the insider is not allowed to keep any part of his illicit profit and, in most cases, to make sure that he yields up a multiple of his profit, perhaps even as much as three times.[25] In the UK, whilst it is difficult to be precise, it would seem that those who have been convicted have fared rather better than their US counterparts. Few have been sentenced to terms of imprisonment, and even fewer have actually gone to prison. Indeed, it is the perception, and no doubt the reality, that economic crime pays as a high-reward and very low-risk endeavour, which has encouraged so many serious and even organised criminals into this area of activity.

An illustration of what some would consider a 'devastating' penalty on a convicted insider is the case of *R v Goodman*.[26] Mr Goodman, a former chairman of a public company, was convicted of an offence which Staughton LJ described as being a 'monstrous and scandalous' example of insider trading. As a result, he was disqualified from being a company director under the Company Directors Disqualification Act 1986 for a period of 10 years. The Court of Appeal considered that such an order was appropriate and justified, as insider dealing did involve a crime which could be considered to have been committed 'in connection with the . . . management . . . of a company'. Taking away the prospect of professional employment for a chartered accountant was acknowledged by the court to be a serious punishment, but one deserved on the facts.

NOTES

1   *Report of the Royal Commission on The Stock Exchange* (1878).
2   Most importantly, the Roskill Committee *Report of The Fraud Trial Committee* (HMSO, 1986). See generally: M Levi *Regulating Fraud* (Tavistock, 1987); Leigh *The Control of Commercial Fraud* (Heinemann, 1982); B Rider and E Hew 'The Regulation of Corpora-

tion and Securities Laws in Britain – The Beginning of the Real Debate' (1977) 19 Mal L Rev 144.

3   See, on the powers of the Serious Fraud Office, D Kirk and A Woodcock *Serious Fraud* (Butterworths, 1993) at Ch 2.

4   See generally B Rider and HL Ffrench *The Regulation of Insider Trading* (Macmillan, 1979).

5   See J Naylor 'The use of Criminal Sanctions by UK and US Authorities for Insider Trading' (1990) 11 *Company Lawyer* 53. For a discussion of the cases, see M Ashe and L Counsell *Insider Trading* (Format, 1990) at pp 18 et seq.

6   As to how the Insider Dealing Group interfaces with other agencies involved in policing insider abuse, see n 5 above and the *Report of the House of Commons' Select Committee on Company Investigations* (1990) at p 36.

7   See the evidence submitted to the House of Commons' Select Committee (see n 6 above) by the Department of Trade and Industry in this regard.

8   On the various devices which can be utilised to hide dealings and ownership, see B Rider 'Fei Ch'ien Laundries – The Pursuit of Flying Money' (1992) 1 *Journal of International Planning* 77.

9   *Re an Inquiry under the Company Securities (Insider Dealing) Act 1985* [1987] BCLC 506.

10 See B Rider 'Policing the International Financial Markets: An English Perspective' (1990) XVI *Brooklyn Journal of International Law* 199.

11 See generally D Kirk and A Woodcock *Serious Fraud* (Butterworths, 1993) at pp 258 et seq.

12 See W McLucas, SM De Tore and L Fountain 'Protection from International Fraud' (1992) 13 *Company Lawyer* 203, continued in (1993) 14 *Company Lawyer* 9; and J Naylor 'The Use of Criminal Sanctions by UK and US Authorities for Insider Trading' (1990) 11 *Company Lawyer* 53.

13 Section 21A of the Securities Exchange Act 1934, as amended by the Insider Trading Sanctions Act 1984, permits a court, in an action brought by the SEC, to impose a civil penalty of up to three times the trading gains, or losses avoided, upon a finding that the defendant violated one of the federal laws relating to insider abuse. The penalty is paid to the US Treasury. Note also, in regard to other developments the facilitation of civil enforcement actions in the Insider Trading and Securities Fraud Enforcement Act 1988.

14 See B Rider 'Insider Trading – A Crime of Our Time?' (Stevens, 1989) *Current Legal Problems, Current Developments in Banking and Finance* 63.

15 See p 68.

16 See B Rider 'Combating International Commercial Crime' (1985) 2 LMCLQ 217, and n 10 above.

17 The Government must be congratulated on its efforts to improve the investigation of economic crime in the Criminal Justice Act 1987, rules relating to evidence in the Criminal Justice Act 1988, international co-operation in Criminal Justice (International Co-operation) Act 1990 and in regard to jurisdiction in the CJA 1993.

18 *Report of the Fraud Trial Committee* (HMSO, 1986) at para 1.

19 See B Rider 'Insider Trading' in *Professional Responsibility* (Legal Research Foundation, 1987) at p 73.

20 *Report on Company Investigations* (1990) HC 36, Recommendations 26 and 29.

21 White Paper *Company Investigations* (1990) (Cm 1149) at p 18.

22 See n 13 above.

23 See J Naylor 'The Use of Criminal Sanctions by UK and US Authorities for Insider Trading' (1990) 11 *Company Lawyer* 53 at p 58, referring to correspondence with a senior official of the SFO.

24 B Rider 'The Power of Fear' (1993) 14 *Company Lawyer* 2.

25 See n 13 above.

26 [1993] 2 All ER 789.

APPENDIX 1

CRIMINAL JUSTICE ACT 1993, PART V

PART V
INSIDER DEALING

The offence of insider dealing

52. The offence

(1) An individual who has information as an insider is guilty of insider dealing if, in the circumstances mentioned in subsection (3), he deals in securities that are price-affected securities in relation to the information.

(2) An individual who has information as an insider is also guilty of insider dealing if—

    (a) he encourages another person to deal in securities that are (whether or not that other knows it) price-affected securities in relation to the information, knowing or having reasonable cause to believe that the dealing would take place in the circumstances mentioned in subsection (3); or

    (b) he discloses the information, otherwise than in the proper performance of the functions of his employment, office or profession, to another person.

(3) The circumstances referred to above are that the acquisition or disposal in question occurs on a regulated market, or that the person dealing relies on a professional intermediary or is himself acting as a professional intermediary.

(4) This section has effect subject to section 53.

53. Defences

(1) An individual is not guilty of insider dealing by virtue of dealing in securities if he shows—

    (a) that he did not at the time expect the dealing to result in a profit attributable to the fact that the information in question was price-sensitive information in relation to the securities; or

(b) that at the time he believed on reasonable grounds that the information had been disclosed widely enough to ensure that none of those taking part in the dealing would be prejudiced by not having the information; or

(c) that he would have done what he did even if he had not had the information.

(2) An individual is not guilty of insider dealing by virtue of encouraging another person to deal in securities if he shows—

(a) that he did not at the time expect the dealing to result in a profit attributable to the fact that the information in question was price-sensitive information in relation to the securities; or

(b) that at the time he believed on reasonable grounds that the information had been or would be disclosed widely enough to ensure that none of those taking part in the dealing would be prejudiced by not having the information; or

(c) that he would have done what he did even if he had not had the information.

(3) An individual is not guilty of insider dealing by virtue of a disclosure of information if he shows—

(a) that he did not at the time expect any person, because of the disclosure, to deal in securities in the circumstances mentioned in subsection (3) of section 52; or

(b) that, although he had such an expectation at the time, he did not expect the dealing to result in a profit attributable to the fact that the information was price-sensitive information in relation to the securities.

(4) Schedule 1 (special defences) shall have effect.

(5) The Treasury may by order amend Schedule 1.

(6) In this section references to a profit include references to the avoidance of a loss.

Interpretation

54. Securities to which Part V applies

(1) This Part applies to any security which—

(a) falls within any paragraph of Schedule 2; and

(b) satisfies any conditions applying to it under an order made by the Treasury for the purposes of this subsection;

and in the provisions of this Part (other than that Schedule) any reference to a security is a reference to a security to which this Part applies.

(2) The Treasury may by order amend Schedule 2.

55. 'Dealing' in securities

(1) For the purposes of this Part, a person deals in securities if—

(a) he acquires or disposes of the securities (whether as principal or agent); or

   (b) he procures, directly or indirectly, an acquisition or disposal of the securities by any other person.

(2) For the purposes of this Part, 'acquire', in relation to a security, includes—

   (a) agreeing to acquire the security; and
   (b) entering into a contract which creates the security.

(3) For the purposes of this Part, 'dispose', in relation to a security, includes—

   (a) agreeing to dispose of the security; and
   (b) bringing to an end a contract which created the security.

(4) For the purposes of subsection (1), a person procures an acquisition or disposal of a security if the security is acquired or disposed of by a person who is—

   (a) his agent,
   (b) his nominee, or
   (c) a person who is acting at his direction,

in relation to the acquisition or disposal.

(5) Subsection (4) is not exhaustive as to the circumstances in which one person may be regarded as procuring an acquisition or disposal of securities by another.

56. 'Inside information', etc

(1) For the purposes of this section and section 57, 'inside information' means information which—

   (a) relates to particular securities or to a particular issuer of securities or to particular issuers of securities and not to securities generally or to issuers of securities generally;
   (b) is specific or precise;
   (c) has not been made public; and
   (d) if it were made public would be likely to have a significant effect on the price of any securities.

(2) For the purposes of this Part, securities are 'price-affected securities' in relation to inside information, and inside information is 'price-sensitive information' in relation to securities, if and only if the information would, if made public, be likely to have a significant effect on the price of the securities.

(3) For the purposes of this section 'price' includes value.

57. 'Insiders'

(1) For the purposes of this Part, a person has information as an insider if and only if—

   (a) it is, and he knows that it is, inside information; and
   (b) he has it, and knows that he has it, from an inside source.

(2) For the purposes of subsection (1), a person has information from an inside source if and only if—

    (a) he has it through—

    (i) being a director, employee or shareholder of an issuer of securities; or

    (ii) having access to the information by virtue of his employment, office or profession; or

    (b) the direct or indirect source of his information is a person within paragraph (a).

58. Information 'made public'

(1) For the purposes of section 56, 'made public', in relation to information, shall be construed in accordance with the following provisions of this section; but those provisions are not exhaustive as to the meaning of that expression.

(2) Information is made public if—

    (a) it is published in accordance with the rules of a regulated market for the purpose of informing investors and their professional advisers;
    (b) it is contained in records which by virtue of any enactment are open to inspection by the public;
    (c) it can be readily acquired by those likely to deal in any securities—

    (i) to which the information relates; or
    (ii) of an issuer to which the information relates; or

    (d) it is derived from information which has been made public.

(3) Information may be treated as made public even though—

    (a) it can be acquired only by persons exercising diligence or expertise;
    (b) it is communicated to a section of the public and not to the public at large;
    (c) it can be acquired only by observation;
    (d) it is communicated only on payment of a fee; or
    (e) it is published only outside the United Kingdom.

59. 'Professional intermediary'

(1) For the purposes of this Part, a 'professional intermediary' is a person—

    (a) who carries on a business consisting of an activity mentioned in subsection (2) and who holds himself out to the public or any section of the public (including a section of the public constituted by persons such as himself) as willing to engage in any such business; or
    (b) who is employed by a person falling within paragraph (a) to carry out any such activity.

(2) The activities referred to in subsection (1) are—

    (a) acquiring or disposing of securities (whether as principal or agent); or
    (b) acting as an intermediary between persons taking part in any dealing in securities.

(3) A person is not to be treated as carrying on a business consisting of an activity mentioned in subsection (2)—

(a) if the activity in question is merely incidental to some other activity not falling within subsection (2); or

(b) merely because he occasionally conducts one of those activities.

(4) For the purposes of section 52, a person dealing in securities relies on a professional intermediary if and only if a person who is acting as a professional intermediary carries out an activity mentioned in subsection (2) in relation to that dealing.

60. Other interpretation provisions

(1) For the purposes of this Part, 'regulated market' means any market, however operated, which, by an order made by the Treasury, is identified (whether by name or by reference to criteria prescribed by the order) as a regulated market for the purposes of this Part.

(2) For the purposes of this Part an 'issuer', in relation to any securities, means any company, public sector body or individual by which or by whom the securities have been or are to be issued.

(3) For the purposes of this Part—

(a) 'company' means any body (whether or not incorporated and wherever incorporated or constituted) which is not a public sector body; and

(b) 'public sector body' means—

(i) the government of the United Kingdom, of Northern Ireland or of any country or territory outside the United Kingdom;

(ii) a local authority in the United Kingdom or elsewhere;

(iii) any international organisation the members of which include the United Kingdom or another member state;

(iv) the Bank of England; or

(v) the central bank of any sovereign State.

(4) For the purposes of this Part, information shall be treated as relating to an issuer of securities which is a company not only where it is about the company but also where it may affect the company's business prospects.

Miscellaneous

61. Penalties and prosecution

(1) An individual guilty of insider dealing shall be liable—

(a) on summary conviction, to a fine not exceeding the statutory maximum or imprisonment for a term not exceeding six months or to both; or

(b) on conviction on indictment, to a fine or imprisonment for a term not exceeding seven years or to both.

(2) Proceedings for offences under this Part shall not be instituted in England and Wales except by or with the consent of—

(a) the Secretary of State; or

(b) the Director of Public Prosecutions.

(3) In relation to proceedings in Northern Ireland for offences under this Part, subsection (2) shall have effect as if the reference to the Director of Public Prosecutions were a reference to the Director of Public Prosecutions for Northern Ireland.

62. Territorial scope of offence of insider dealing

(1) An individual is not guilty of an offence falling within subsection (1) of section 52 unless—

- (a) he was within the United Kingdom at the time when he is alleged to have done any act constituting or forming part of the alleged dealing;
- (b) the regulated market on which the dealing is alleged to have occurred is one which, by an order made by the Treasury, is identified (whether by name or by reference to criteria prescribed by the order) as being, for the purposes of this Part, regulated in the United Kingdom; or
- (c) the professional intermediary was within the United Kingdom at the time when he is alleged to have done anything by means of which the offence is alleged to have been committed.

(2) An individual is not guilty of an offence falling within subsection (2) of section 52 unless—

- (a) he was within the United Kingdom at the time when he is alleged to have disclosed the information or encouraged the dealing; or
- (b) the alleged recipient of the information or encouragement was within the United Kingdom at the time when he is alleged to have received the information or encouragement.

63. Limits on section 52

(1) Section 52 does not apply to anything done by an individual acting on behalf of a public sector body in pursuit of monetary policies or policies with respect to exchange rates or the management of public debt or foreign exchange reserves.

(2) No contract shall be void or unenforceable by reason only of section 52.

64. Orders

(1) Any power under this Part to make an order shall be exercisable by statutory instrument.

(2) No order shall be made under this Part unless a draft of it has been laid before and approved by a resolution of each House of Parliament.

(3) An order under this Part—

- (a) may make different provision for different cases; and
- (b) may contain such incidental, supplemental and transitional provisions as the Treasury consider expedient.

SCHEDULE 1

SPECIAL DEFENCES

Market makers

1.—(1) An individual is not guilty of insider dealing by virtue of dealing in securities or encouraging another person to deal if he shows that he acted in good faith in the course of —
  (a) his business as a market maker, or
  (b) his employment in the business of a market maker.

(2) A market maker is a person who —
  (a) holds himself out at all normal times in compliance with the rules of a regulated market or an approved organisation as willing to acquire or dispose of securities; and
  (b) is recognised as doing so under those rules.

(3) In this paragraph "approved organisation" means an international securities self-regulating organisation approved under paragraph 25B of Schedule 1 to the Financial Services Act 1986.

Market information

2.—(1) An individual is not guilty of insider dealing by virtue of dealing in securities or encouraging another person to deal if he shows that —
  (a) the information which he had as an insider was market information; and
  (b) it was reasonable for an individual in his position to have acted as he did despite having that information as an insider at the time.

(2) In determining whether it is reasonable for an individual to do any act despite market information at the time, there shall, in particular, be taken into account –
  (a) the content of the information;
  (b) the circumstances in which he first had the information and in what capacity; and
  (c) the capacity in which he now acts.

3. An individual is not guilty of insider dealing by virtue of dealing in securities or encouraging another person to deal if he shows —
  (a) that he acted —
    (i) in connection with an acquisition or disposal which was under consideration or the subject of negotiation; or in the course of a series of such acquisitions or disposals; and
    (ii) with a view to facilitating the accomplishment of the acquisition or disposal or the series of acquisitions or disposals; and

(b)   that the information which he had as an insider was market information arising directly out of his involvement in the acquisition or disposal or series of acquisitions or disposals.

4. For the purposes of paragraphs 2 and 3 market information is information consisting of one or more of the following facts —

(a)   that securities of a particular kind have been or are to be acquired or disposed of, or that their acquisition or disposal is under consideration or the subject of negotiation;

(b)   that securities of a particular kind have not been or are not to be acquired or disposed of;

(c)   the number of securities acquired or disposed of or to be acquired or disposed of or whose acquisition or disposal is under consideration or the subject of negotiation;

(d)   the price (or range of prices) at which securities have been or are to be acquired or disposed of or the price (or range of prices) at which securities whose acquisition or disposal is under consideration or the subject of negotiation may be acquired or disposed of;

(e)   the identity of the persons involved or likely to be involved in any capacity in an acquisition or disposal.

Price stabilisation

5.—(1) An individual is not guilty of insider dealing by virtue of dealing in securities or encouraging another person to deal if he shows that he acted in conformity with the price stabilisation rules.

(2) In this paragraph "the price stabilisation rules" means rules which –

(a)   are made under section 48 of the Financial Services Act 1986 (conduct of business rules); and

(b)   make provision of a description mentioned in paragraph (i) of subsection (2) of that section (price stabilisation rules).

SCHEDULE 2

SECURITIES

Shares

1. Shares and stock in the share capital of a company ("shares").

Debt securities

2. Any instrument creating or acknowledging indebtedness which is issued by a company or public sector body, including, in particular, debentures, debenture stock, loan stock, bonds and certificates of deposit ("debt securities").

Warrants

3. Any right (whether conferred by warrant or otherwise) to subscribe for shares or debt securities ("warrants").

Depositary receipts

4.—(1) The rights under any depositary receipt.

(2) For the purposes of sub-paragraph (1) a "depositary receipt" means a certificate or other record (whether or not in the form of a document) —
- (a) which is issued by or on behalf of a person who holds any relevant securities of a particular issuer; and
- (b) which acknowledges that another person is entitled to rights in relation to the relevant securities or relevant securities of the same kind.

(3) In sub-paragraph (2) "relevant securities" means shares, debt securities and warrants.

Options

5. Any option to acquire or dispose of any security falling within any other paragraph of this Schedule.

Futures

6.—(1) Rights under a contract for the acquisition or disposal of relevant securities under which delivery is to be made at a future date and at a price agreed when the contract is made.

(2) In sub-paragraph (1) —
- (a) the references to a future date and to a price agreed when the contract is made include references to a date and a price determined in accordance with terms of the contract; and
- (b) "relevant securities" means any security falling within any other paragraph of this Schedule.

Contracts for differences

7.—(1) Rights under a contract which does not provide for the delivery of securities but whose purpose or pretended purpose is to secure a profit or avoid a loss by reference to fluctuations in —
- (a) a share index or other similar factor connected with relevant securities;
- (b) the price of particular relevant securities; or
- (c) the interest rate offered on money placed on deposit.

(2) In sub-paragraph (1) "relevant securities" means any security falling within any other paragraph of this Schedule.

APPENDIX 2

THE INSIDER DEALING (REGULATED MARKETS AND SECURITIES) ORDER 1993 (DRAFT)

Made   *1993*
Coming into force   *1993*

Whereas a draft of this Order has been approved by a resolution of each House of Parliament pursuant to section [   ] of the Criminal Justice Act 1993;

Now, therefore, the Treasury, in exercise of the powers conferred on them by sections [and   and   ] of that Act and of all other powers enabling them in that behalf, hereby make the following Order:-

1. This Order may be cited as the Insider Dealing (Regulated Markets and Securities) Order 1993 and shall come into force on   1993.

Regulated markets

2. The following markets are regulated markets for the purposes of Part IV of the Criminal Justice Act 1993 (insider dealing) –

(a) any market which is established under the rules of an investment exchange specified in Part I of the Schedule to this Order; and

(b) any market which meets the criteria specified in Part II of that Schedule.

Securities

3. Articles 4 to 6 set out conditions for the purposes of section 31(1) of the Act of 1993 (securities to which Part IV applies).

4. The following condition applies in relation to any security which falls within any paragraph of Schedule [   ] to the Act of 1993, that is, that it is dealt in on or under the rules of, or has its price quoted on, a regulated market.

5. The following alternative condition applies in relation to warrants, that is, that the rights under it are rights to subscribe for any share or debt security which satisfies the condition in article 4.

6. The following alternative condition applies in relation to a depositary receipt, that is, that the rights under it are in respect of any share or debt security which satisfies the condition in article 4.

7. The following alternative conditions apply in relation to an option or a future, that is, that the options or rights under it are in respect of —
  (a)   any share or debt security which satisfies the condition in article 4, or
  (b)   any depositary receipt which satisfies the condition in article 4 or article 6.

8. The following alternative condition applies in relation to a contract for differences, that is, that the purpose or pretended purpose of a contract for differences is to secure a profit or avoid a loss by reference to fluctuations in –
  (a)   the price of any shares or debt securities which satisfy the condition in article 4, or
  (b)   an index of the price of such shares or debt securities.

United Kingdom regulated markets

9. The regulated markets which are regulated in the United Kingdom for the purposes of Part IV of the Act of 1993 are any market which is established under the rules of –
  (a)   the International Stock Exchange of the United Kingdom and the Republic of Ireland Limited, other than the market which operates in the Republic of Ireland known as the Irish Unit of the International Stock Exchange of the United Kingdom and the Republic of Ireland Limited;
  (b)   London International Financial Futures Exchange (Administration & Management); and
  (c)   OM (London) Limited.

1993.   Two of the Lord Commissioners
                                                  of Her Majesty's Treasury.

SCHEDULE   Article 2

REGULATED MARKETS
PART I

Amsterdam Stock Exchange.
Antwerp Stock Exchange.
Athens Stock Exchange.
Barcelona Stock Exchange.

Bavarian Stock Exchange.
Berlin Stock Exchange.
Bilbao Stock Exchange.
Bologna Stock Exchange.
Bordeaux Stock Exchange.
Bremen Stock Exchange.
Brussels Stock Exchange.
Copenhagen Stock Exchange.
Dusseldorf Stock Exchange.
Florence Stock Exchange.
Frankfurt Stock Exchange.
Genoa Stock Exchange.
Ghent Stock Exchange.
Hamburg Stock Exchange.
Hanover Stock Exchange.
The International Stock Exchange of the United Kingdom and the Republic of Ireland Limited.
Liège Stock Exchange.
Lille Stock Exchange.
Lisbon Stock Exchange.
London International Financial Futures Exchange (Administration & Management).
Luxembourg Stock Exchange.
Lyon Stock Exchange.
Madrid Stock Exchange.
Marseille Stock Exchange.
Milan Stock Exchange.
Munich Stock Exchange.
Nancy Stock Exchange.
Nantes Stock Exchange.
Naples Stock Exchange.
The exchange known as NASDAQ.
OM (London) Limited.
Oporto Stock Exchange.
Palermo Stock Exchange.
Paris Stock Exchange.
Rome Stock Exchange.
Stuttgart Stock Exchange.
Trieste Stock Exchange.
Turin Stock Exchange.
Valencia Stock Exchange.
Venice Stock Exchange.

PART II

The criteria in relation to markets for the purposes of article 2 of this Order are that –
  (a) the head office of the investment exchange under the rules of which the market is established is situated in a member State; and

(b)   the market is subject to requirements in the member State in which that head office is situated as to –
- (i)   the manner in which it operates;
- (ii) the means by which access may be had to the facilities it provides;
- (iii) the conditions to be satisfied before a security may be dealt in by means of, or before its price may be quoted on, its facilities, and
- (iv) the reporting and publication of dealing effected by means of its facilities.

THE TRADED SECURITIES (DISCLOSURE) REGULATIONS 1993 (DRAFT)

Made	*1993*
Laid before Parliament	*1993*
Coming into force	*1993*

Whereas the Treasury are a government department designated for the purposes of section 2(2) of the European Communities Act 1972 in relation to measures relating to the publication of information about developments in the sphere of activity of a company or undertaking, whose securities are admitted to trading on a market, which may affect the price of that company's or undertaking's securities;

Now, therefore, the Treasury in exercise of the powers conferred on them by section 2(2) of that Act hereby make the following Regulations:-

Citation and commencement

1.—(1) These Regulations may be cited as the Traded Securities (Disclosure) Regulations 1993.

(2) These Regulations shall come into force on   1993.

Interpretation

2. In these Regulations:-

"the Official List" has the meaning given by section 142(7) of the Financial Services Act 1986;

"recognised investment exchange" has the meaning given by section 207(1) of the Financial Services Act 1986;

"regulated market" means any market in the United Kingdom on which securities are admitted to trading being a market which is regulated and supervised by a recognised investment exchange and which operates regularly and is accessible directly or indirectly to the public; and

"security" means any security which falls within any paragraph of the Schedule to these Regulations but does not include an investment falling within paragraph 1 of Schedule 1 to the Financial Services Act 1986 which is admitted to the Official List in accordance with the provisions of Part IV of that Act and the expressions "admitted to trading" and "company or undertaking" have the same meaning as in the Council Directive co-ordinating regulations on insider dealing (No.89/592/EEC)

Obligation to disclose information

3.—(1) A company or undertaking which is an issuer of a security admitted to trading on a regulated market (an "issuer") shall inform the public as soon as possible of any major new developments in the issuer's sphere of activity which are not public knowledge and which may, by virtue of their effect on the issuer's assets and liabilities or financial position or on the general course of its business, lead to substantial movements in the price of that security.

(2) A recognised investment exchange which regulates and supervises a regulated market on which an issuer's securities are admitted to trading may exempt the issuer from the obligation imposed by paragraph (1) above if satisfied that the disclosure of the particular information would prejudice the legitimate interests of that issuer.

(3) The rules of a recognised investment exchange must, at least, enable the exchange, in the event of a failure by an issuer whose securities are admitted to trading on a regulated market which the exchange regulates and supervises to comply [with][1] the obligation imposed by paragraph (1) above, either –

    (a)   to publish the fact that the issuer concerned has failed to comply with the requirement; and

    (b)   itself to make public any information which that issuer has failed to publish.

4. The Financial Services Act 1986 shall have effect as if the requirement set out in paragraph (3) of regulation 3 above was –

    (a)   in the case of a recognised investment exchange which is not an overseas investment exchange within the meaning of section 207(1) of that Act, among those specified in Schedule 4 to that Act (requirements for recognition of investment exchange); and

    (b)   in the case of an investment exchange which is an overseas investment exchange within the meaning of section 207(1) of that Act, among those specified in section 40(2) of that Act (overseas investment exchange and clearing houses).

1993   Two of the Lords Commissioners
of Her Majesty's Treasury

---

1 With respect, the authors have inserted the word 'with' on the assumption that the draft omitted it in error.

SCHEDULE   Regulation 2

1. Shares and stock in the share capital of a company ("shares").

2. Any instrument creating or acknowledging indebtedness which is issued by a company or undertaking, including, in particular, debentures, debenture stock, loan stock, bonds and certificates of deposit ("debt securities").

3. Any right (whether conferred by a warrant or otherwise) to subscribe for shares or debt securities ("warrants").

4.—(1) The rights under any depositary receipt.

(2) For the purposes of sub-paragraph (1) a "depositary receipt" means a certificate or other record (whether or not in the form of a document) –
   (a)   which is issued by or on behalf of a person who holds any relevant securities of a particular issuer; and
   (b)   which acknowledges that another person is entitled to rights in relation to the relevant securities or relevant securities of the same kind.

(3) In sub-paragraph (2) "relevant securities" means shares, debt securities and warrants.

5. Any option to acquire or dispose of any security falling within any other paragraph of this Schedule.

6.—(1) Rights under a contract for the acquisition of relevant securities for delivery at a future date and at a price agreed upon when the contract is made.

(2) In sub-paragraph (1) "relevant securities" means any security falling within any other paragraph of this Schedule.

7.—(1) Rights under a contract which does not provide for the delivery of securities but whose purpose or pretended purpose is to secure a profit or avoid a loss –
   (a)   by reference to fluctuations in –
      (i)   a share index or other factor connected with relevant securities; or
      (ii)   the price of particular relevant securities; and
   (b)   not by acquiring or disposing of the shares or the relevant securities themselves.

(2) In sub-paragraph (1) "relevant securities" means any security falling within any other paragraph of this Schedule.

APPENDIX 3

THE MODEL CODE

Introduction (not forming part of the Model Code)

The freedom of directors and certain employees of listed companies to deal in their company's securities is restricted in a number of ways – by statute, by common law and by the requirement of the listing rules that listed companies adopt and apply a code of dealing based on the *Model Code* set out in this appendix. This requirement imposes restrictions beyond those that are imposed by law. Its purpose is to ensure that directors, certain employees and persons connected with them (within the meaning of section 346 of the Companies Act 1985) do not abuse, and do not place themselves under suspicion of abusing, price-sensitive information that they may have or be thought to have, especially in periods leading up to an announcement of results.

The main headings of the *Model Code* for transactions in securities by directors, certain employees and persons connected with them are:

definitions
dealings by directors and relevant employees
- purpose of dealing
- dealing in close periods
- dealing in other circumstances
- dealing in another company's securities
- clearance to deal
- circumstances for refusal
- dealing in exceptional circumstances
- director acting as trustee
dealings by connected persons and investment managers
list of dealings
special circumstances
- exercise of options
- personal equity plans
- savings schemes etc.
- guidance on other dealings
relevant employees.

Definitions

1. In this code the following definitions apply unless the context otherwise requires:

(a) 'close period' means any of the periods when a director is prohibited from dealing as specified in paragraph 3 of this code;

(b) 'dealing' includes any sale or purchase of, or agreement to sell or purchase, any securities and the grant, acceptance, acquisition, disposal, exercise or discharge of an option (whether for the call, or put, or both) or other right or obligation, present or future, conditional or unconditional, to acquire or dispose of securities or any interest in securities;

(c) 'prohibited period' means any period to which paragraph 7 of this code applies;

(d) 'relevant employee' means any employee of the listed company or director or employee of a subsidiary undertaking or parent undertaking of the listed company who, because of his office or employment in the listed company or subsidiary undertaking or parent undertaking, is likely to be in possession of unpublished price-sensitive information in relation to the listed company;

(e) 'securities' means any listed securities and, where relevant, securities which have been designated for trading on the Unlisted Securities Market (the 'USM');

(f) 'unpublished price-sensitive information' in relation to any securities of a company is information which:

   (i) relates to specific matters relating, or of concern (directly or indirectly), to that company, that is to say, is not of a general nature relating, or of concern, to that company; and

   (ii) is not generally known to those persons who are accustomed or would be likely to deal in those securities but which would, if it were generally known to them, be likely materially to affect the price of those securities:

and it should be assumed without prejudice to the generality of the above that any information regarding transactions required to be notified to the Company Announcements Office in accordance with chapter 10 or chapter 11 of the listing rules and information of the kind referred to in the paragraphs of the listing rules set out below is price-sensitive:

Paragraph

9.1	general obligation of disclosure
9.10(a)	alterations to capital structure
9.11 and 9.12	notification of major interests in shares
15.1 and 15.9	purchase of own securities
16.13 and 16.15	notification of directors' interests.

Dealings by directors and relevant employees

Purpose of dealing

2. A director must not deal in any securities of the listed company on considerations of a short term nature.

Dealing in close periods

3. A director must not deal in any securities of the listed company during a 'close period'. A close period is:
  (a) the period of two months immediately preceding the preliminary announcement of the company's annual results or, if shorter, the period from the relevant financial year end up to and including the time of the announcement; and
  (b) if the company reports on a half-yearly rather than a quarterly basis, the period of two months immediately preceding the announcement of the half-yearly results or, if shorter, the period from the relevant financial period end up to and including the time of the announcement; or
  (c) if the company reports on a quarterly basis, the period of one month immediately preceding the announcement of the quarterly results or, if shorter, the period from the relevant financial period end up to and including the time of the announcement (save that for the final quarter paragraph 3(a) of this code applies).

Dealing in other circumstances

4. A director must not deal in any securities of the listed company at any time when he is in possession of unpublished price-sensitive information in relation to those securities, or otherwise where clearance to deal is not given under paragraph 7 of this code.

Dealing in another company's securities

5. A director must not deal in any securities of another listed or USM company at any time when he is in possession of unpublished price-sensitive information by virtue of his position as a director, or as an employee of the listed company or any subsidiary undertaking or parent undertaking of the listed company, in relation to those securities.

Clearance to deal

6. A director must not deal in any securities of the listed company without advising the chairman (or one or more other directors designated for this purpose) in advance and receiving clearance. In his own case, the chairman, or other designated director, must advise the board in advance at a board meeting, or advise another designated director, and receive clearance from the board or designated director, as appropriate.

Circumstances for refusal

7. A director must not be given clearance (as required by paragraph 6 of this code) to deal in any securities of the listed company during a prohibited period. A 'prohibited period' means:
  (a) any close period;
  (b) any period when there exists any matter which constitutes unpublished price sensitive information in relation to the company's securities (whether or not the director has knowledge of such matter) and the proposed dealing

would (if permitted) take place after the time when it has become reasonably probable that an announcement will be required in relation to that matter; or

(c)   any period when the person responsible for the clearance otherwise has reason to believe that the proposed dealing is in breach of this code.

8. A written record must be maintained by the company of the receipt of any advice received from a director pursuant to paragraph 6 of this code and of any clearance given. Written confirmation from the company that such advice and clearance (if any) have been recorded must be given to the director concerned.

Dealing in exceptional circumstances

9. In exceptional circumstances clearance may be given for a director to sell (but not to purchase) securities when he would otherwise be prohibited from doing so only because the proposed sale would fall within a close period. Clearance may not, however, be given if the chairman or designated director is aware of any other reason why the director would be prohibited from dealing by this code. An example of the type of circumstance which may be considered exceptional for these purposes would be a pressing financial commitment on the part of the director that cannot otherwise be satisfied. The determination of whether circumstances are exceptional for this purpose must be made by the person responsible for the clearance.

Director acting as trustee

10. Where a director is a sole trustee (other than a bare trustee), the provisions of this code will apply, as if he were dealing on his own account. Where a director is a co-trustee (other than a bare trustee), he must advise his co-trustees of the name of the listed company of which he is a director. If he is not a beneficiary, a dealing in his company's securities undertaken by that trust will not be regarded as a dealing by the director for the purposes of this code, where the decision to deal is taken by the other trustees acting independently of the director or by investment managers on behalf of the trustees. The other trustees will be assumed to have acted independently of the director for this purpose where they:

(a)   have taken the decision to deal by a majority without consultation with, or other involvement of, the director concerned; or

(b)   if they have delegated the decision making to a committee of which the director is not a member.

Dealings by connected persons and investment managers

11. A director must (so far as is consistent with his duties of confidentiality to his company) seek to prohibit (by taking the steps set out in paragraph 12 of this code) any dealing in securities of the listed company during a close period or at a time when the director is in possession of unpublished price sensitive information in relation to those securities and would be prohibited from dealing under paragraph 7(b) of this code:

(a)   by or on behalf of any person connected with him (within the meaning of section 346 of the Companies Act 1985); or

(b) by an investment manager on his behalf or on behalf of any person connected with him whether either he or any person connected with him has funds under management with that investment manager, whether or not discretionary (save as provided in paragraphs 10 and 16 of this code).

12. For the purposes of paragraph 11 of this code, a director must advise all such connected persons and investment managers:

(a) of the name of the listed company of which he is a director;

(b) of the close periods during which they cannot deal in the company's securities;

(c) of any other periods when the director knows he is not himself free to deal in securities of the company under the provisions of this code unless his duty of confidentiality to the company prohibits him from disclosing such periods; and

(d) that they must advise him immediately after they have dealt in securities of the company (save as provided in paragraphs 10 and 16 of this code).

List of dealings

13. A list of dealings in the securities of the company since the date of the previous list should be circulated to members of the board with the board papers for each board meeting where such dealings are:

(a) by or on behalf of a director;

(b) by connected persons of a director; or

(c) by investment managers on behalf of either a director or a connected person of a director (unless paragraph 10 or 16 of this code applies).

Special circumstances

Exercise of options

14. The chairman or other designated director may allow the exercise of an option or right under an employees' share scheme which has been approved by shareholders, or the conversion of a convertible security, where the final date for the exercise of such option or right, or conversion of such security, falls during any prohibited period and the director could not reasonably have been expected to exercise it at an earlier time when he was free to deal.

15. Where an exercise or conversion is permitted pursuant to paragraph 14 of this code, the chairman or other designated director may not, however, give clearance for the sale of securities acquired pursuant to such exercise or conversion.

Personal equity plans

16. A director may enter into a discretionary personal equity plan without regard to the provisions of this code save that, in the case of a single company personal equity plan, the provisions of paragraph 17 of this code apply.

17. A director may enter into a single company personal equity plan which involves regular payments by standing order or direct debit of sums which are to be invested only in securities of the listed company if the following provisions are complied with:

   (a)   he does not enter into the plan or carry out the first purchase of the securities of the listed company within the plan during a prohibited period;

   (b)   he does not cancel or vary the terms of his participation, or carry out sales of the securities of the listed company within the plan during a prohibited period; and

   (c)   before entering into the plan or cancelling the plan or varying the terms of his participation or carrying out sales of the securities of his company within the plan, he obtains clearance under paragraph 6 of this code.

Savings schemes etc.

18. A director may enter into a scheme under which securities of his company:

   (a)   are purchased pursuant to a regular standing order or direct debit arrangement;

   (b)   are acquired by way of a standing election to reinvest dividends or other distributions received; or

   (c)   are acquired pursuant to a standing election to receive shares in place of a cash dividend:

if the provisions set out in paragraph 17 of this code in relation to single company personal equity plans are complied with.

Guidance on other dealings

19. For the avoidance of doubt, the following constitute dealings for the purposes of this code and are consequently subject to the provisions of this code:

   (a)   arrangements which involve a sale of securities with the intention of repurchasing an equal number of such securities soon afterwards ('bed and breakfast') dealings);

   (b)   dealings between directors and/or relevant employees of the company;

   (c)   transfers of shares already held into a discretionary personal equity plan by means of a matched sale and purchase; and

   (d)   off-market dealings.

20. For the avoidance of doubt, and notwithstanding the definition of dealing contained in paragraph 1(b) of this code, the following dealings are not subject to the provisions of this code:

   (a)   undertakings to take up entitlements under a rights issue or other offer;

   (b)   the take up of entitlements under a rights issue or other offer;

   (c)   allowing entitlements to lapse under a rights issue or other offer;

   (d)   the sale of sufficient entitlements nil-paid to allow take up of the balance of the entitlements under a rights issue;

   (e)   undertakings to accept, or the acceptance of, a takeover offer; and

   (f)   a dealing by a director with a person whose interest in securities is to be treated by virtue of section 328 of the Companies Act 1985 (extension of section 324 to spouses and children) as the director's interest.

Relevant employees

21. Relevant employees must comply with the terms of this code as though they were directors.

The text of the Model Code for securities transactions by directors of listed companies has been reproduced from *The Listing Rules* with the kind permission of the Board of the International Stock Exchange of the United Kingdom and the Republic of Ireland Limited. Those readers who need to consult the rules should refer to *The Listing Rules* which is available from The Stock Exchange.

APPENDIX 4

COUNCIL DIRECTIVE COORDINATING REGULATIONS ON INSIDER DEALING (89/592/EEC)

THE COUNCIL OF THE EUROPEAN COMMUNITIES,

Having regard to the Treaty establishing the European Economic Community, and in particular Article 100a thereof,

Having regard to the proposal from the Commission,

In cooperation with the European Parliament,

Having regard to the opinion of the Economic and Social Committee,

Whereas Article 100a (1) of the Treaty states that the Council shall adopt the measures for the approximation of the provisions laid down by law, regulation or administrative action in Member States which have as their object the establishment and functioning of the internal market;

Whereas the secondary market in transferable securities plays an important role in the financing of economic agents;

Whereas, for that market to be able to play its role effectively, every measure should be taken to ensure that market operates smoothly;

Whereas the smooth operation of that market depends to a large extent on the confidence it inspires in investors;

Whereas the factors on which such confidence depends include the assurance afforded to investors that they are placed on an equal footing and that they will be protected against the improper use of inside information;

Whereas, by benefiting certain investors as compared with others, insider dealing is likely to undermine that confidence and may therefore prejudice the smooth operation of the market;

Whereas the necessary measures should therefore be taken to combat insider dealing;

Whereas in some Member States there are no rules or regulations prohibiting insider dealing and whereas the rules or regulations that do exist differ considerably from one Member State to another;

Whereas it is therefore advisable to adopt coordinated rules at a Community level in this field;

Whereas such coordinated rules also have the advantage of making it possible, through cooperation by the competent authorities, to combat transfrontier insider dealing more effectively;

Whereas, since the acquisition or disposal of transferable securities necessarily involves a prior decision to acquire or to dispose taken by the person who undertakes one or other of these operations, the carrying-out of this acquisition or disposal does not constitute in itself the use of insider information;

Whereas insider dealing involves taking advantage of inside information; whereas the mere fact that market-makers, bodies authorized to act as *contrepartie*, or stockbrokers with insider information confine themselves, in the first two cases, to pursuing their normal business of buying or selling securities or, in the last, to carrying out an order should not in itself be deemed to constitute use of such inside information; whereas likewise the fact of carrying out transactions with the aim of stabilizing the price of new issues or secondary offers of transferable securities should not in itself be deemed to constitute use of inside information;

Whereas estimates developed from publicly available data cannot be regarded as inside information and whereas, therefore, any transaction carried out on the basis of such estimates does not constitute insider dealing within the meaning of this Directive;

Whereas communication of inside information to an authority, in order to enable it to ensure that the provisions of this Directive or other provisions in force are respected, obviously cannot be covered by the prohibitions laid down by this Directive,

HAS ADOPTED THIS DIRECTIVE:

Article 1

For the purposes of this Directive:

1 'inside information' shall mean information which has not been made public of a precise nature relating to one or several issuers of transferable securities or to one or several transferable securities, which, if it were made public, would be likely to have a significant effect on the price of the transferable security or securities in question;

2 'transferable securities' shall mean:

    (a) shares and debt securities, as well as securities equivalent to shares and debt securities;

    (b) contracts or rights to subscribe for, acquire or dispose of securities referred to in (a);

    (c) futures contracts, options and financial futures in respect of securities referred to in (a);

(d) index contracts in respect of securities referred to in (a),

when admitted to trading on a market which is regulated and supervised by authorities recognized by public bodies, operates regularly and is accessible directly or indirectly to the public.

Article 2

1. Each Member State shall prohibit any person who:

— by virtue of his membership of the administrative, management or supervisory bodies of the issuer,

— by virtue of his holding in the capital of the issuer, or

— because he has access to such information by virtue of the exercise of his employment, profession or duties,

possesses inside information from taking advantage of that information with full knowledge of the facts by acquiring or disposing of for his own account or for the account of a third party, either directly or indirectly, transferable securities of the issuer or issuers to which that information relates.

2. Where the person referred to in paragraph 1 is a company or other type of legal person, the prohibition laid down in that paragraph shall apply to the natural persons who take part in the decision to carry out the transaction for the account of the legal person concerned.

3. The prohibition laid down in paragraph 1 shall apply to any acquisition or disposal of transferable securities effected through a professional intermediary.

Each Member State may provide that this prohibition shall not apply to acquisitions or disposals of transferable securities effected without the involvement of a professional intermediary outside a market as defined in Article 1 (2) *in fine*.

4. This Directive shall not apply to transactions carried out in pursuit of monetary, exchange-rate or public debt-management policies by a sovereign State, by its central bank or any other body designated to that effect by the State, or by any person acting on their behalf. Member States may extend this exemption to their federated States or similar local authorities in respect of the management of their public debt.

Article 3

Each Member State shall prohibit any person subject to the prohibition laid down in Article 2 who possesses inside information from:

(a) disclosing that inside information to any third party unless such disclosure is made in the normal course of the exercise of his employment, profession or duties;

(b) recommending or procuring a third party, on the basis of that inside information, to acquire or dispose of transferable securities admitted to trading on its securities markets as referred to in Article 1 (2) *in fine*.

Article 4

Each Member State shall also impose the prohibition provided for in Article 2 on any person other than those referred to in that Article who with full knowledge of the facts possesses inside information, the direct or indirect source of which could not be other than a person referred to in Article 2.

Article 5

Each Member State shall apply the prohibitions provided for in Articles 2, 3 and 4, at least to actions undertaken within its territory to the extent that the transferable securities concerned are admitted to trading on a market of a Member State. In any event, each Member State shall regard a transaction as carried out within its territory if it is carried out on a market, as defined in Article 1 (2) *in fine*, situated or operating within that territory.

Article 6

Each Member State may adopt provisions more stringent than those laid down by this Directive or additional provisions, provided that such provisions are applied generally. In particular it may extend the scope of the prohibition laid down in Article 2 and impose on persons referred to in Article 4 the prohibitions laid down in Article 3.

Article 7

The provisions of Schedule C.5 (a) of the Annex to Directive 79/279/EEC shall also apply to companies and undertakings the transferable securities of which, whatever their nature, are admitted to trading on a market as referred to in Article 1 (2) *in fine* of this Directive.

Article 8

1. Each Member State shall designate the administrative authority or authorities competent, if necessary in collaboration with other authorities to ensure that the provisions adopted pursuant to this Directive are applied. It shall so inform the Commission which shall transmit that information to all Member States.

2. The competent authorities must be given all supervisory and investigatory powers that are necessary for the exercise of their functions, where appropriate in collaboration with other authorities.

Article 9

Each Member State shall provide that all persons employed or formerly employed by the competent authorities referred to in Article 8 shall be bound by professional secrecy. Information covered by professional secrecy may not be divulged to any person or authority except by virtue of provisions laid down by law.

Article 10

1. The competent authorities in the Member States shall cooperate with each other whenever necessary for the purpose of carrying out their duties, making use of the powers mentioned in Article 8 (2). To this end, and notwithstanding Article 9, they shall exchange any information required for that purpose, including information relating to actions prohibited, under the options given to Member States by Article 5 and by the second sentence of Article 6, only by the Member State requesting cooperation. Information thus exchanged shall be covered by the obligation of professional secrecy to which the persons employed or formerly employed by the competent authorities receiving the information are subject.

2. The competent authorities may refuse to act on a request for information:

(a) where communication of the information might adversely affect the sovereignty, security or public policy of the State addressed;
(b) where judicial proceedings have already been initiated in respect of the same actions and against the same persons before the authorities of the State addressed or where final judgment has already been passed on such persons for the same actions by the competent authorities of the State addressed.

3. Without prejudice to the obligations to which they are subject in judicial proceedings under criminal law, the authorities which receive information pursuant to paragraph 1 may use it only for the exercise of their functions within the meaning of Article 8 (1) and in the context of administrative or judicial proceedings specifically relating to the exercise of those functions. However, where the competent authority communicating information consents thereto, the authority receiving the information may use it for other purposes or forward it to other States' competent authorities.

Article 11

The Community may, in conformity with the Treaty, conclude agreements with non-member countries on the matters governed by this Directive.

Article 12

The Contact Committee set up by Article 20 of Directive 79/279/EEC shall also have as its function:

(a) to permit regular consultation on any practical problems which arise from the application of this Directive and on which exchanges of view are deemed useful;

(b) to advise the Commission, if necessary, on any additions or amendments to be made to this Directive.

Article 13

Each Member State shall determine the penalties to be applied for infringement of the measures taken pursuant to this Directive. The penalties shall be sufficient to promote compliance with those measures.

Article 14

1. Member States shall take the measures necessary to comply with this Directive before 1 June 1992. They shall forthwith inform the Commission thereof.

2. Member States shall communicate to the Commission the provisions of national law which they adopt in the field governed by this Directive.

Article 15

This Directive is addressed to the Member States.

INDEX